SHORT COURSE SERIES

Clockwise

upper-intermediate

Classbook

Jon Naunton

OXFORD
UNIVERSITY PRESS

Contents

PEOPLE

01 YOURS INSINCERELY p.4

Listening / Pronunciation
Focusing on social exchanges.
'Mirroring' with enthusiastic intonation.

English in use
Expressions for party talk (introductions, offers and invitations etc.).
Responding to what's been said (*Neither can I, So do we*).

Speak out
Roleplay. Meeting new people at a party.

02 PERSONAL PROFILES p.7

Grammar
Linking past and present.
Ever / never + superlatives.

Reading / Vocabulary
Looking at obsessions.
Setting reading goals.

Listening / Pronunciation
Showing enthusiasm, responding to the speaker.
Weak forms.

Speak out
Roleplay. Talking about a hobby.

03 FIXING YOU UP p.10

Listening / Vocabulary
Different views of a relationship.
Phrases related to relationships.

English in use
Saying what you think.

Reading
Finding a partner. Predicting the contents of a text.
Four types of multi-word verbs.

Speak out
Pair / group work. Ranking factors for successful relationships and agreeing.

04 FAMILY LIFE p.13

Vocabulary
Multi-word verbs related to families (*get on with, take after*).
Family relationship words (*only child, sibling*).

Reading
Jigsaw reading. Looking at family relationships.
Expressions with *keep* (*keep an eye on, keep cool*).

Speak out
Class survey. Talking about families and upbringing.

PLACES

05 HOME TOWN p.15

Listening
Following someone talking about where they come from.

English in use / Pronunciation
Responding in a conversation.
Sounding interested using short questions and enthusiastic intonation.

Key word
Expressions with *like* (*Would you like to ...? What's it like?*)

Speak out
Group work. Talking about your home town.

06 HAPPY TOGETHER p.18

Listening
Following and taking notes on people talking about an unusual community.

Grammar
Modals of obligation, permission, and necessity (*can't, have to*, etc.).
Permit, oblige, require, and *forbid*.

Speak out
Group work. Talking about lifestyles, rules, and regulations in three different places.

07 POLITENESS PAYS p.21

Reading
Looking at standards of politeness.

Listening
Listening to different requests.

English in use
Being polite. Softening requests and replies.

Speak out
Group work. A board game to practise making requests.

08 AS I REMEMBER p.24

Reading
Childhood memories.
Used to and *would* for past habits and states.

Vocabulary
Remember, remind, and *forget*.
Words related to memory (*memorize, reminder*).

Speak out
Pair / group work. Talking about childhood memories.

STORIES

09 IT HAPPENED TO ME p.26

Listening
Following the stages of a story.

Vocabulary / Pronunciation
Multi-word verbs related to driving (*slow down, run over*).
Extreme adjectives (*delicious, gorgeous*).
Using emphatic stress.

English in use
Participating during storytelling.

Speak out
Group work. Telling a personal anecdote.

10 DRIVING PASSIONS p.29

Reading
Driving stories. Skimming a text for gist.

Grammar
Past narrative tenses.
Then, after that, after and *afterwards*.

Speak out
Group work. Telling personal anecdotes about driving experiences.

11 HIGHLY RECOMMENDED p.32

Vocabulary
Words associated with taste (*sweet, spicy*). Adjectives used to describe films, books, etc. (*gripping, tedious*).

Reading
Three reviews.

Listening
Recommending kinds of entertainment.

English in use / Pronunciation
Making recommendations (*It's on at ..., You should see it ...*).
Using exaggerated intonation.

Speak out
Pair / group work. Giving personal reviews.

12 SAME BUT DIFFERENT p.35

Reading
Re-assembling a jumbled text about a linguistically embarrassing situation.

Vocabulary
False friends and words which are easily confused (*library / bookshop, diary / agenda*).

Key word
Expressions with *mind* (*Mind out! Never mind*).

Speak out
Pair / group work. Telling anecdotes.

WORK

13 GETTING THROUGH p.37

Reading
Looking at formality. Picking up on tone.

Vocabulary
Multi-word verbs related to telephoning (*cut off, look up*).

Listening
Dealing with different callers.

English in use
Expressions which reflect levels of formality.

Speak out
Roleplay. Telephone conversations.

14 INTO THE FUTURE p.40

Listening
Following five everyday situations.

Grammar
Ways of expressing the future.
Adjectival phrases (*bound to, likely to*).

Speak out
Group work. Ranking the likelihood of future events occurring.

15 DRESS FOR SUCCESS p.43

Listening
Following advice on interviews.

Key word
Multi-word verbs and patterns with *look* (*look up to, look like*).

Reading / Vocabulary
An article about dressing for work.
Looking at different adjectives to describe image.

English in use
Dealing with interview questions.

Speak out
Roleplay. Doing a job interview.

16 CATS AND RATS p.46

Reading
Looking at a text about work and salaries. Job titles and status.

Vocabulary
Adjectives to describe jobs (*stressful, rewarding*). Noun phrases (*application form, overtime*) and expressions (*to be made redundant, to pull strings*).

Speak out
Pair work. Looking at a text about an unusual job. Discussion about unemployment.

GLOBAL CULTURE

17 GOING PLACES p.48
Reading/Vocabulary
Scanning a holiday brochure.
Confusing words (*excursion/journey*).
Listening
Following a discussion about a tour. Focusing on colloquial lexical phrases in context (*keen on, do your own thing*).
English in use
Suggestions and preferences.
Verb forms (*-ing* form or infinitive).
Asserting yourself.
Speak out
Group work. Making suggestions, asserting your own point of view, agreeing.

18 ALL THE BEST p.51
Reading
Evaluating a text about tourists.
Adjectives to describe national characteristics.
Grammar
Comparatives and superlatives.
Modifiers and quantifiers.
Listening
Following an anecdote about a hotel.
Speak out
Group work. Inventing stories around picture prompts.

19 SO MANY QUESTIONS p.54
Listening
Understanding tone.
English in use
Forming indirect questions.
Evasive answers.
Reading
An interview. Matching questions and answers.
Speak out
Pair work. Asking personal questions.

20 WHO DO YOU THINK YOU ARE? p.57
Vocabulary/Pronunciation
Adjectives describing character and attitudes.
Word stress patterns.
Reading
A magazine article about opinions from different cultures.
Speak out
Pair work. Deciding where to live.

HUMAN INVENTION

21 FESTIVAL p.59
Listening
Following a talk and note-taking.
English in Use
Language signals (*Anyway ...,
You see ...*) and repetition (*fewer and fewer*).
Key word
Expressions with *take*
(*take advantage of, take part in*).
Speak out
Group work. Giving a talk about a special event.

22 EUREKA! p.62
Reading
Exchanging information/completing notes.
Words and phrases related to the innovation of a product.
Grammar
Form and uses of the passive.
The causative *have* and *get*.
Speak out
Group work. Describing how a product was invented and promoting its benefits.

23 A GOLDEN AGE? p.65
Listening
Following a guided tour.
English in Use
Expressions for showing people around.
Key word
Different meanings of *get* (*get hurt, get worse*).
used to + base form/*used to* + *-ing* form.
Speak out
Group work. Planning the stages of a guided tour.

24 THE WAY TO DO IT p.68
Vocabulary
Technology and computing vocabulary.
Listening
Understanding and giving instructions.
Expressions to describe position (*inside out, upside down*).
Speak out
Pair work. Practising giving and carrying out instructions.

ISSUES

25 INSTANT OPINIONS p.70
Reading
Understanding word play in headlines. Reading between the lines.
Listening
Following the reactions of different people to newspaper stories.
English in use
Ways of giving opinions, contradicting, reacting, and drawing similarities.
Key word
Expressions with *thing* (*The thing is ..., that's the main thing*).
Speak out
Group work. Discussing and giving opinions.

26 THE GREATEST HOAX OF ALL? p.73
Listening
Following a conversation about the moon landings.
Grammar
Modals of deduction and speculation.
Speak out
Group work. Talking about the story behind the picture. Using language of speculation.

27 IT'S MY LIFE p.76
Reading
Looking for opinions expressed in a text about a schoolgirl model.
Vocabulary
Focusing on multi-word verbs in context.
Listening
Following people having a heated discussion.
English in use/Pronunciation
Expressing blame (*should/ought to have done*) Expressions with *on earth* (*What/How on earth ...?*).
Using emphatic stress.
Speak out
Group work. Ranking and discussion exercise.

28 LIGHTING A CANDLE p.79
Vocabulary
The vocabulary of headlines.
Word-building: nouns from adjectives (*poor/poverty*).
Listening
Following two people discussing a charity.
Words in context from a brochure (*civilians, casualties*).
Speak out
Group work. Discussing and agreeing.

SOCIAL ROLES

29 RUMOURS p.81
Listening
Following two conversations about gossip.
English in use/Pronunciation
Expressions for gossiping
(*You'll never guess what I've heard, I won't breathe a word*).
Looking at intonation and voice range.
Speak out
Pair work/whole class activity.
Exchanging rumours.

30 TRADING PLACES p.84
Reading
Making notes on a text about gender swapping.
Grammar
Hypothesizing. First, second, third, and mixed conditionals.
Forms of *wish*.
Listening
Following three people talking about what/who they would like to have been.
Speak out
Pair/group work. Talking about regrets.

31 REPUTATIONS p.87
Reading
Interpreting different views of a teacher.
Listening
Following four conversations and how different people interact.
English in use
Focusing on conversational techniques.
Speak out
Pair work. Discussing and agreeing on an evening's entertainment.

32 FOLLOW YOUR DREAM p.90
Reading
Ranking qualities for successful business people. Reading about a successful business.
Vocabulary
Recording and classifying different types of multi-word verbs.
Listening
Following the story of a business success.
Speak out
Pair work. Ordering a picture story.

PRACTICE p.92   **EXTRA ACTIVITIES** p.108   **TAPESCRIPTS** p.112

01 YOURS INSINCERELY

In this lesson

- Look at how to get to know people when you meet them for the first time.
- Focus on useful expressions for introductions, offers, and invitations.
- Practise responding to what someone has just said.

Text A

The beauty of flattery is that it's so easy. Say anything favourable that comes into your head. You cannot go too far with flattery, if you want to be polite. Tell people they're brilliant, beautiful, important, accomplished, and good. This is known as lying.

P.J. O'Rourke

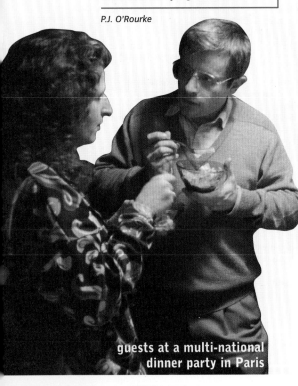

guests at a multi-national dinner party in Paris

Speak for yourself

1 Find a partner you don't already know.
   1 Introduce yourself.
   2 Find out three things about them.

2 In pairs, decide ...
   1 how you felt in this situation. Rate yourself from 1 (nervous) to 5 (confident).
   2 how good you are at meeting and getting to know new people.
   3 whether you know anyone who is very confident in new situations.

3 Think of some good ways to start conversations with people you don't know.

4 Quickly read the three extracts.

Text B

Six ways to make people like you:
1 be genuinely interested in other people
2 smile
3 remember that a person's name is to that person the sweetest and most important sound in any language
4 be a good listener
5 encourage others to talk about themselves
6 talk in terms of the other person's interests

Make the other person feel important – and do it sincerely.

Dale Carnegie

Text C

A good, all-purpose opening technique is, 'Tell me ...', pause, look attentively, then put a question that seems likely to suit. It doesn't matter whether it's, 'If you could retire tomorrow what would you do?', or 'What is it like to be the Head of the Pentagon?', or 'How come your children are so good?'. Listen to the answer, pick out something interesting and say, 'That's very interesting, so you ...', and repeat the point. That makes the speaker feel understood and appreciated. So he will elaborate. You can keep this up with tiny variations for hours.

Moyra Bremner

   1 In pairs, note down the techniques suggested.
   2 Decide on the most useful. Which, if any, do you use?

5 Do you think it's possible to learn to be a more successful person from a book?

Listening
Social exchanges

 1 Listen to Conversation 1. Complete Column 1.

Conversation	1	2	3
1 What is the conversation about?			
2 How do they feel about each other?			
3 Which techniques do they use?			

> One way of keeping a conversation going is by 'mirroring', i.e. repeating something the other person says with enthusiastic intonation. This makes you sound interested.

2 Listen again. Then in pairs, practise this extract.

Fiona	Well, I'm a professional ice-skater …
Victor	An ice-skater. That's very interesting …
Fiona	… and I'm in a competition next week.
Victor	A competition!

3 Practise mirroring. Find out from other people about …
* where they're from.
* their job.
* their hobbies.
* their family.

 4 Listen to Conversations 2 and 3. Complete the chart in ex.1 above.

English in use
Party talk

1 Listen to all three conversations again. Note expressions for …

* introductions.

* offers and invitations.

* expressing disappointment.

* ending conversations.

* leave-taking.

2 Check with the Tapescript on *p.112*.

3 In pairs, add other expressions.

Responding to what's been said

4 Respond to these statements.

1 I can't stand her work. *Neither can I.*
2 I don't usually enjoy parties.
3 I hope we can get together again soon.
4 I'm not tired.
5 We're staying at the Majestic Hotel.
6 I've been to the Empire State Building.
7 We really enjoyed the holiday.
8 I'd like to stay longer.

 5 Listen and copy the intonation.

6 Write five true sentences about yourself. In pairs, take turns to read and respond. Agree where appropriate.

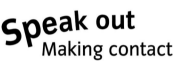
Speak out
Making contact

1 Read about Jim Haynes and answer questions 1 to 3.

Would anyone out there like to meet an American called Jim Haynes?

I'm talking about the Jim Haynes who lives in Atelier A-2, Rue de la Tombe Issoire, Paris 75014, and whose telephone number is 00 33 1 4327 1767.

If you're not interested, you should be ashamed. Because Jim Haynes is one of the friendliest people on earth. He would certainly want to meet you. Not only is he willing to have his address and telephone number published, but he would like you to come for dinner with him one Sunday night the next time you are in Paris. Just give him a ring the previous Saturday to check that his guest list of fifty has not already been exceeded. He has been holding his public dinner parties every Sunday for well over twenty years and is still as keen as ever.

If you do go, you will find that the other guests will all be there for the express purpose of meeting each other. Beyond that they will have nothing in common at all. They will all be strangers, as will Jim Haynes himself. But by the end of the evening another fifty people from around the globe will have made some progress along the road of getting to know the world better.

The Independent on Sunday

Think before you speak

* Think about how to make contact with each new person.
* Be interested in the other person. Ask them about themselves (job, interests, family etc.). Use their name.
* Be a good listener. Smile, flatter, sound enthusiastic. Practise 'mirroring'.
* Use the language you have studied for introductions, offers, invitations, ending conversations, and leave-taking.

1 What do you think has motivated him for the past twenty years?
2 Would you go to one of his parties?
3 Why aren't there more people who are ready to do this?

2 You are at one of Jim Haynes's parties. Everyone you are about to meet is new.

* Mix with the other guests and make contact.
* Find out as much about each other as you can. Find out what you have in common.
* Talk to at least four different people.

02 PERSONAL PROFILES

In this lesson

- Revise and extend uses of the present perfect simple and continuous.
- Use active listening in conversation.
- Practise talking to someone about a special interest.

Speak for yourself

1 On average, how long do you spend each week on …?

- your personal appearance
- a hobby or pastime
- a sport or keeping fit
- work or study

2 What do people often become obsessed by? Note three ideas under each heading.

| TEENAGERS | MIDDLE-AGED PEOPLE | THE ELDERLY |

Reading
Setting goals

Effective reading

Set clear reading goals when reading magazine articles or stories.

- Before you read, ask yourself what you would like to find out.
- Don't try to understand every word; just find answers to the questions you have set yourself.

1 In pairs, **A** read Text A, **B** read Text B. Complete the chart for your text. Exchange information with your partner.

	Text A	Text B
1 the obsession		
2 when/how it started		
3 what motivates them		
4 the effect it has on their life		

2 Highlight words/phrases which show the level of their obsessions.
Micki – *I couldn't give up the job.*

3 Talk again to a partner about the obsessions of Micki Pistorious, Michael Bane, or someone you know. Use at least three expressions from the texts.

Text A

Micki Pistorious is South Africa's only forensic psychologist. Since 1994 she has compiled psychological profiles on at least eight serial killers. Her greatest triumph to date has been her role in the capture of Cape Town's 'Station Strangler' who had killed twenty-two boys. The police had made no progress in catching him since he first struck in 1986 so they called in Micki. 'I said he'd be in his late twenties, a teacher or a policeman who lived with his folks, very neat, and with a decent car.' The profile led to Norman Simon, a 28-year-old teacher.

Micki's marriage has become a casualty of her career. 'I thought it would be unfair to stay married. I can be away for weeks on end. But I couldn't give up the job. The 'high', the feeling of satisfaction you get when you've helped detectives find a serial killer, is unbelievable. It's addictive.' However, she has no social life outside work, and spends weekends alone reading about serial killers.

She magazine

Text B

Michael Bane was a 39-year-old wimp when he began an epic journey through the world of extreme sports. Ever since he was caught in a frightening storm one day while windsurfing, he just can't get enough of danger. Since then he has taken up thirteen extreme sports ranging from skydiving to ice-climbing. He has taken part in a downhill mountain bike race at night, and paddled over a waterfall. 'There's never a time that's so clear as when failure in what you're doing can mean your death', he said. 'You are more focused and intense, and you can bring that into the things you do every day.'

One benefit is that he can keep office stress in proportion. 'After being trapped for seven days in a snowstorm in Alaska I have a good idea of what a bad day is.' Familiarity with danger creates a fierce desire for risk. 'It becomes so commonplace that you look for something new to test yourself', Bane believes. The price of being hooked on risk is high. In the past month he has lost one friend on a deep dive in Egypt and another in white water in Colorado.

The Sunday Times

Forms of the present perfect

Grammar revisited

1 Correct these sentences. Explain why they are wrong.

1 A few years ago he has been trapped in a snowstorm.

2 She is a forensic psychologist since 1986.

3 Did you ever go sky-diving? No, never.

4 Did you see that film yet?

5 Sorry I'm late. Have you waited a long time?

6 So far, she has been helping them to solve more than twelve crimes.

7 How long have you been knowing Michael?

8 I'm studying English since I was at school.

2 Check your answers in the Summary on *p.9*.

Grammar plus

> **The present perfect simple can also be used:**
> • with superlative constructions.
> *That was the best meal I've ever eaten.*
> • when a clause begins with *this / that / it + be + the first / second*, etc. *time.*
> *This is the second time I've been to England.*
>
> **The present perfect continuous can also be used:**
> • to describe the present visible results of a past activity.
> *Have you been crying? Your eyes are all red.*
> • to talk about a series of repeated but finished actions leading up to the present.
> *I've been trying to ring all morning but his number is always engaged.*

3 Complete the sentences. Use the verbs in brackets.

1 'Is this the first time you _____ (eat) here?' 'And the last. I don't think I _____ (ever have) such an awful meal.'

2 Jill looks like a tomato because she _____ (sunbathe) by the pool all day.

3 This is the second time I _____ (go) to Florence. I love it here.

4 I _____ (tell) him to clear up his room all week but it doesn't make any difference. I think I _____ (ask) him about twenty times.

5 'You're out of breath. What _____ (you do)?'
'I _____ (chop) wood for the fire all morning.'

Against the clock!

Set a time limit _____

4 In pairs, complete the text. Use the verbs in brackets.

> One day, Alfred David's wife **1**_____ (tell) him that he walked like a penguin. Since then, his identification with the creatures **2**_____ (become) almost total. For the past twenty-five years he **3**_____ (walk) around in a penguin suit. People in his home town in Belgium long ago **4**_____ (accept) this harmless eccentric as part of the scenery. All this time, he **5**_____ (collect) penguin objects, and so far he **6**_____ (accumulate) over two thousand. A few years ago he **7**_____ (open) the European Museum of the Penguin. As far as anyone knows, he **8**_____ (never go) to Antarctica but this **9**_____ (not stop) him from making friends among the penguin population. Since his fascination **10**_____ (develop) he **11**_____ (buy) tons of fish to feed his 'friends and family' in the local zoo. If he looks more and more like one it could be because he **12**_____ (eat) too much raw fish himself.
>
> **PENGUIN MAN**

Listening
Active listening

1 Listen to Justin, who collects Swatch watches, talking to Saskia. Why are these numbers and times important?

| 98 | 12 years ago | 24 hours | £1,000 | £50,000 |

2 Listen again. How does Justin show his enthusiasm for his hobby?

3 How does Saskia show that she is actively listening to what Justin says? Find examples in the Tapescript on *pp.112 / 113*.

4 Listen and copy the intonation. What happens to the words in italics?

   1 So how long *have* you *been* collecting them, Justin?

   2 *For* about eleven or twelve years, I suppose.

   3 I used *to* travel a lot with my job.

   4 I thought they *were* bright *and* cheerful.

   5 Sometimes it's hard *to* choose.

5 In pairs find out about your partner's hobbies or pastimes. Tell the rest of the class.

Speak out
Talking about a hobby

1 In pairs, look at the two pictures. Then **A** turn to *p.108*, **B** to *p.110*. Complete the notes about your person's hobby.

	Tom Payne	Louise Wilkinson
• their normal job		
• what the hobby is		
• how long they've been doing it		
• when they normally do it		
• what it involves		
• if it needs any special clothes/equipment		
• if it involves other people		

Think before you speak

- Use present perfect simple and continuous constructions correctly.
- Use weak forms as naturally as you can.
- Communicate your enthusiasm about your hobby.
- Show that you are actively listening to the other person.

2 Imagine that you are the person in the text you read. Interview each other. Find out as much as you can.

SUMMARY

The present perfect simple

Form

subject + *have/has* + past participle
He **has** *just* **arrived**.

Use

- to talk about a completed action or experience in the past without saying exactly when it happened.
I've been to Germany three times.
With a finished past time expression, use the past simple.
I went to Germany last week/two years ago/in 1980.
- when something which started in the past continues up to the present.
They've lived in the same house for thirty years.
- to talk about recent events.
I've just bought a new car.
- when a past action is visible in the present.
Your hair looks nice. Have you been to the hairdresser's?

The present perfect continuous

Form

subject + *have / has been* + present participle
He **has been living** here since May.

Use

- if we want to focus more on the extended action than the result.
I feel exhausted because I've been working hard all day.
When there is a focus on completion, use the present perfect simple.
I've finished that book. I really enjoyed it.
- if we want to suggest that something is temporary.
I've been staying with my sister for the last couple of weeks.
- to talk about repeated actions and events.
I've been playing a lot of tennis recently.
When the number of times an action has occurred is specified, use the present perfect simple.
I've already had three coffees this morning.

03
FIXING YOU UP

In this lesson

- Practise giving your opinion about different kinds of relationships.
- Extend your vocabulary to do with relationships.
- Look briefly at the four types of multi-word verbs.

Speak for yourself

1 Look at the percentages for how couples meet in Sweden.
   1 Is there anything that you find surprising?
   2 Guess the statistics for your own country.

2 Think of a couple you know well. Tell a partner how they met.

HOW 100 COUPLES MET	at a dance or night club	in a public place or festival	at work	at private homes or parties	on holiday or a trip	during their studies	by being neighbours	through a dating agency	other	TOTAL
SWEDEN %	24	18	14	12	10	8	3	1	10	100
YOUR COUNTRY %										

Reading

Using titles and opening sentences

1 Look at the title. What do you think the article will be about?

Effective reading

When you read, use titles and opening sentences to help you unlock the meaning of the text.

- Titles usually describe the overall topic of the article which follows.
- The first sentence of a paragraph often introduces or summarizes the rest.

Singapore fixes you up

a — Like many women she feels ready to settle down as she approaches thirty. She has experienced more than a little family pressure about still being single at her age. And it is not only her family but also her government who are keen for her to marry and reproduce.

b — Her salary as a radio executive means she can drive a luxury car and go shopping. Singapore's government believes that, to ensure continuous prosperity, future generations must become more intelligent. And it is concerned that female graduates – ideal for breeding this super-race – are staying single and childless. Singapore's men, on the other hand, are marrying less educated women. So the government has launched a campaign to encourage the 'right' couples to get together.

c — This is partly because high pressure jobs leave little time for socializing and meeting potential partners. In Singapore, the problem is made worse by cultural traditions. The sexes are not encouraged to mix during childhood or to date until after university.

d — 'There's a first time for everything,' he says. Like Madeline he has signed up with the SDU (Social Development Unit), the government's very own dating agency. The SDU is open only to graduates, who sign up for five years, although most members are married within three.

e — In one, a young man sits on a park bench, sighing, 'Where is my dream girl?' At the other end, a girl stares into space thinking, 'Where is the man of my dreams?' They fail to notice each other and wander off, lonely. A voice-over warns, 'Why not reality? You could wait a lifetime for a dream.'

She magazine

2 Read the 'opening sentences' below. Match them to paragraphs **a** to **e**.

1 Putting off marriage and parenthood is becoming more common in all industrialized nations.   Paragraph ☐

2 Government-sponsored ads on prime time TV aim to get the message across.   Paragraph ☐

3 Living in one of the world's most successful economies, Madeline has had a good education and the pick of jobs.   Paragraph ☐

4 Research scientist Kee-Chuan Goh (29) has never had a girlfriend.   Paragraph ☐

5 It's Friday night in Singapore and, once again, Madeline Tan (28) doesn't have a date.   Paragraph ☐

3 Read the text again. Write 'true' or 'false'.

1 The greatest pressure to marry has come from Madeline's parents.

2 Women graduates make popular wives.

3 It's hard for men and women to mix naturally.

4 Adverts encourage young people to have more realistic expectations.

4 How well would this kind of 'social engineering' work in your country?

Multi-word verbs

Remember the four basic types of multi-word verb.

1 Those which don't take an object (intransitive).
*It's time you **settled down**.*

2 Those which can be separated by their object (separable).
*In Singapore young professionals **put marriage off** / **put it off** until they are older.*

3 Those which can't be separated by their object (inseparable).
*I **bumped into him** three years later.* NOT *I ~~bumped him into~~.*

4 Three part multi-word verbs (inseparable).
*I **get on with** her really well.*

Archie's first wife, Linda

Archie and his second wife, Janet

Listening
Friends and relationships

🔊 1

1 Work in two groups. Listen to the tape. Group **A** make notes about Janet. Group **B** make notes about Linda.

	Janet	Linda
• relationship to Archie		
• how they met		
• the relationship's early stages		
• what other people thought		
• how the relationship developed		
• what can be learnt from this		

2 With a partner from the other group, use your notes to retell the story you heard.

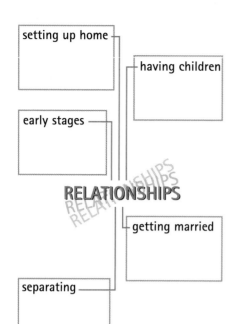

setting up home

having children

early stages

RELATIONSHIPS

getting married

separating

3 In pairs, refer to the Tapescript on *p.113*. Add appropriate words/ phrases to the 'Relationships' spidergram. Add at least two words of your own to each category.

4 Look at the types of multi-word verb on *p.11*. What type are the verbs in your spidergram?

English in use
Saying what you think

Giving opinions

Personally, I think … it was best for both of them.
I definitely think / believe … you can get married too young, you know.
Another thing is, …
People should (never) … rush into marriage.
Everyone ought to … live together first.

Giving examples

Take (Archie and Linda) for instance …

Personal reactions

We were amazed when …   People couldn't believe it when …
I just knew …   I was absolutely astonished …
I wasn't surprised when …

1 Write five true sentences using phrases from the box.

2 Talk about a couple you know, and their relationship.

Speak out
Making it last

1 Look at the following ingredients for long and successful relationships.
   1 Decide on your top five and rank them in order.
   2 Compare with a partner.

Think **before you speak**

- Use a wide variety of vocabulary to describe relationships.
- Use a range of expressions to say what you think.
- Support your opinions with examples of people you know.
- Include your/other people's reactions to events.
- Use different types of multi-word verbs accurately.

Long-lasting relationship

ingredients   *serves 2*

- financial security
- mutual physical attraction
- shared interests and hobbies
- similar race and religion
- roughly similar ages
- being able to laugh together

- similar social/economic backgrounds
- similar physical appearance/attractiveness
- similar educational background/intelligence
- children
- shared political views
- similar attitudes towards money

2 In groups of four, agree on the three most important and the three least important considerations.

04 FAMILY LIFE

In this lesson

- Extend your vocabulary to do with family relationships.
- Practise multi-word verbs to do with upbringing.
- Focus on expressions with *keep*.

do something suspicious
    or naughty
force someone to leave
become older and stop doing
    something
respect and admire
die
match or fulfil

Speak for yourself

1 What are the following?

> a nuclear family   an extended family   a single parent family

2 Describe other family units you know. Which are the most common in your country?

3 In Nigeria, people say 'it takes a whole village to raise a child'. What do you think they mean by this?

Vocabulary

Family relationships

1 Give a definition for the multi-word verbs in **bold**.
   1 I didn't **get on with** my father when I was young.
     get on with = have a good relationship with
   2 She certainly **takes after** her grandmother; she's got the same quick temper!
   3 Could you **look after** the children while I go shopping?
   4 What terrible table manners! I blame the parents for **bringing** him **up** so badly.
   5 She's just a selfish child. It's time she **grew up**.
   6 Her parents **told** her **off** for coming home after midnight.

2 Match the multi-word verbs with the phrases in the box.
   1 I've always felt guilty for not **living up to** my parents' expectations.
   2 The children are very quiet. They must be **getting up to** something.
   3 Jack cries all night long. I hope he'll **grow out of** it.
   4 They've threatened to **kick** me **out** because they don't like my boyfriend.
   5 It was a terrible shock because I had always **looked up to** my father.
   6 I was very sad to hear that your grandmother had **passed away**.

3 Work in two groups, **A** and **B**.

   1 **Against the clock!** Explain the words in your box in five minutes.

A		
an only child	a bachelor	a mummy's boy
a granny	a dutiful daughter	a sugar daddy
a spinster	your mum and dad	kids
a spoilt brat	an auntie	next of kin

B		
a black sheep	siblings	a half-sister
relations / relatives	a spouse	your partner
your mother-in-law	a stepsister	a foster-brother
a great-grandfather	a godmother	dependants

   2 Test a partner from the other group.
   3 Decide which of the words in the box ...
     - are formal / informal / neutral.
     - have a negative connotation.

Text A

How far should a daughter live from her elderly parents? This is a question which has occupied some of the best minds in Japan. Obviously the best way of keeping an eye on them is if they live next door. However, this might not be so good for the rest of the family. Living in the next city is the mark of an uncaring daughter; cruellest of all is to live in another country. No, apparently the maximum distance a dutiful daughter should live from her folks is two blocks. This is based on the 'miso soup' test. If we imagine that both she and her parents live on the middle floor of different apartment buildings, the boiling miso soup she takes them has the chance to cool down a little, but should keep pleasantly hot until it reaches them.

Reading
Words in context

1 In two groups, **A** and **B**, read some key words from your text. Try to predict the content. Read your text and check.

Text A		
daughter	parents	Japan
distance	soup	

Text B		
Italian	mother	son
Rome	shirts	

Text B

If anything, Italy's low birth rate has strengthened the ties between Italian mothers and their sons. When twenty-seven-year-old Giancarlo Brunetti finally went to work in Rome, his mother made him promise to send his washing home each week. Every Friday he sends it by bus to Bari in southern Italy. On Sunday evening, after a round trip of 800 km, Giancarlo picks up his freshly-washed and ironed shirts. 'It's a way of keeping in touch. My girlfriend Luisa keeps calling me a mummy's boy, but I don't care. Mum's happier, it makes my life easier, and I keep my word,' he says, unashamedly.

Time magazine

2 Tell a partner from the other group about your text.

3 What do you think of the parent / child relationships described? Talk about one you know.

4 Find *keep* expressions in the texts. Complete the sentences with similar expressions.

  1 If you watch over someone you _____ .

  2 In summer the fridge _____ .

  3 If you do what you agreed to do then you _____ .

  4 I was bullied at school. The other kids _____ .

  5 A good way of _____ is by writing letters.

Speak out
Keep it in the family

1 List five words/expressions for family members under each heading.

PARENTS	SIBLINGS	EXTENDED FAMILY

2 Ask other students about their families. Start with these questions.

  1 Where were you born and brought up?

  2 Who, if anyone, do you take after?

  3 Who looked after you?

  4 How well do / did you get on with your family?

  5 How conventional was your upbringing?

Think before you speak

- Use as much new vocabulary to describe your family as you can.

- Include multi-word verbs to do with upbringing.

05
HOME TOWN

In this lesson

- Practise talking about where you come from.
- Look at how to keep a conversation going using short questions and enthusiastic intonation.
- Use expressions with the key word *like*.

Speak for yourself

1 [🔊1] Listen to four people listing things that remind them of their home towns. Guess where they are from.

1 😐 _____   2 😕 _____   3 😐 _____   4 😕 _____

2 Do the same for your home town. Explain your choice of words.

Listening
Talking about your roots

1 Look at the information on Salt Lake City. Would you like to visit it?

[🔊2] 2 Listen to **Part A**. Identify labels 1 to 5 on the map.

In the valley of Salt Lake

The **biggest** city between Denver and the Pacific coast

State Capital of Utah

Industries include food, printing, petrol refineries, copper, silver, lead mines

Famous for its huge temple and the Mormon Tabernacle Choir

SaltLakeCity, USA

Founded in 1847 by Brigham Young as the capital of the Mormons (Christian group)

BRIGHAM YOUNG

→ Geography
  Position (north/south/east/west)
  Features (mountains, lake, sea,
  river, valley, etc.)
→ What life was like
  It used to be ... but now ...
  I used to ...
→ What people do for a living
  Farming/industry, etc.
  Companies famous for ... (products)
→ Things to do/see
  Activities (skiing, etc.)
  Sights/interesting places to visit/
  historical associations

3 [○2] Listen to the rest of the interview.
  1 What do you think life was like for a young person growing up in Salt Lake City? Listen to **Part B** and check.
  2 Diana talks about businesses which have moved to Salt Lake City. Listen to **Part C** and complete the sentences.
    1 Salaries _____
    2 American Express _____
    3 IBM is _____
  3 What does the region offer tourists? Listen to **Part D** and check.

4 Use the flowchart. Ask a partner about a place they know. Find out as much as you can.

English in use
Responding with short questions

For conversations to work, both sides need to participate. One way is to react to a statement with a short question form. This encourages the other person to say something extra. Remember to show that you're listening by smiling and keeping eye contact.

[○3]
1 Listen to this extract again.

Diana	I went on holiday there just a few months ago ...	STATEMENT
Julian	Oh, did you?	SHORT QUESTION
Diana	Yes, it was wonderful ...	EXTENSION

  1 What's the relationship between the statement and the question?
  2 What's the intonation pattern of the question?

2 In pairs, practise responding with short questions. Add an extension.
  1 Paul didn't pass his exam again. *Oh, didn't he? Is he going to try again?*
  2 Janet's going to Morocco next spring.
  3 Her brother's a famous sportsman.
  4 I couldn't do the exercise.
  5 They live in a big house in the country.
  6 She had a bad fall when she went skiing.
  7 The postman hasn't been yet.
  8 It's the biggest waterfall in the world.

3 [○4] Look at the dialogue. Listen and copy the intonation patterns.
4 Practise short questions and enthusiastic intonation. In pairs, ask about ...
  • where your partner lives.
  • what they do for a living.
  • their free time.

Short questions and enthusiastic intonation can be combined to make the listener sound interested.
A What do you do in your free time, Ben?
B I like mountaineering.
A Mountaineering?
B Yeah, last year I went to the Himalayas.
A Oh, did you? That sounds fun.
B Yes, it was great ...

Key word

like

1 ... like a big valley.
2 ... like to grow up in?
3 ... like IBM.
4 ... like long fingers
5 I like to ...
6 ... like to go back for good
one day?

1 Look at *like* in sentences 1 to 6 on the left.

   1 Remember and complete. Then check in the Tapescript on *p.113.*

   2 Write 'verb' (V) or 'preposition' (P).

2 Match the questions and answers.

   1 What's she like to work for ?   **a** As long as it's dry.

   2 Would you like a chocolate?   **b** It's got grey and black stripes.

   3 Is your sister like you?   **c** No, thanks. I'm on a diet.

   4 What does your cat look like?   **d** Impossible to please.

   5 Do you like white wine?   **e** No, we're very different.

3 Which question above ... ?

   1 is an offer   ☐

   2 asks about general preferences   ☐

   3 asks about someone's character   ☐

   4 asks about similarities   ☐

   5 asks for a physical description   ☐

4 Against the clock! In pairs, make as many questions / sentences with *like* as you can in three minutes.

Speak out
Where you come from

In groups, talk about where you come from. Cover as many topics as you can.

Where were you brought up?

tourist sights

famous people

Where were you born?

important industries

historical events / places

something people are proud of

food and drink, local specialities

folklore / festivals

How old were you when you moved to your town?

Think before you speak

• Talk about different aspects of home towns: geography, what life is / was like, what people do, things to do / see.

• Be an interested, enthusiastic listener; participate by reacting to what the other person says.

• Use expressions with *like* and other new words to describe towns and cities.

06
HAPPY TOGETHER

In this lesson

- Revise and extend the language of obligation, permission, and necessity.
- Practise talking about rules and regulations.
- Focus on life in some unusual communities.

Speak for yourself

Complete these sentences. Compare with a partner.

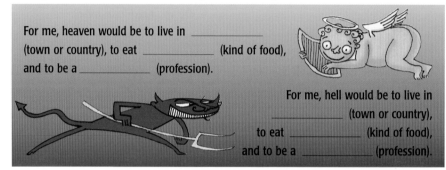

For me, heaven would be to live in _____ (town or country), to eat _____ (kind of food), and to be a _____ (profession).

For me, hell would be to live in _____ (town or country), to eat _____ (kind of food), and to be a _____ (profession).

Listening
Note-taking

1 Read the paragraph below. What do you think of Celebration?

Celebration, near Orlando, is the perfect picture of small-town America. Looking at photographs you would think it had grown slowly over the past hundred years. Instead, it is a great social experiment, the dream of Walt Disney, the founder of the Disney corporation. It opened on November 18th 1995, Mickey Mouse's birthday, and thirty years after Disney's death. Thousands of Americans unhappy with modern city life wanted to move there.

2 Tricia and Larry are talking about Celebration. Listen and make notes about **Part 1**.

Part 1	Part 2
• reasons for living there	• curtains
• kind of people who live there	• cars
• facilities	• house design
	• gardens

3 Listen to **Part 2**. Make notes about the rules in Celebration.

4 Use your notes. Talk in groups about the concept of Celebration.
   1 What do you like / dislike?
   2 Are there any rules you would introduce?
   3 Would you like to live there?

Obligation, permission, and necessity

Grammar revisited

1 Who might be talking in these six situations?

1 **I don't have to** dress smartly and I can come to work when I want.

2 I've told you before. **You mustn't** play with the washing machine!

3 **I have to** look after the children. I also **have to** do a little bit of housework.

4 80 kilos! **I've got to** lose weight before the summer holidays! **I must!**

5 This is the staff room; **you're not supposed to** smoke in here but a lot of people do.

6 **You don't need to** do your homework until Tuesday. Enjoy your weekend!

2 Which of the forms in **bold** do we use ... ?
- to talk about our responsibilities
- to describe rules we should follow but don't always obey
- when something isn't necessary
- for a strong prohibition
- when we tell ourselves something is urgent or necessary
- when there is no obligation to do something

3 Check your answers in the Summary on *p.20*.

4 Look at **Part 2** of the Tapescript on *p.114*. Underline ways of expressing obligation and necessity. Explain why each form is used.

Grammar plus

> **didn't need to** and *needn't have*
> - Use *didn't need to* to explain that you didn't do something because it wasn't necessary.
>   *I didn't need to go to London in the end because the meeting was cancelled.*
> - Use *needn't have* when you <u>did</u> something but realized later that it wasn't necessary.
>   *I needn't have made sandwiches because they'd stopped for lunch on the way.*
>
> **make, let,** and *allow*
> - Use *make* (active or passive) when there is a sense of force.
>   *She made him finish his soup before he could have any ice-cream.*
>   *He was made to sit down and write the letter.*
> - Use *allow* (active or passive) to express permission.
>   *She was allowed to go to the party.*
>   *Her parents allowed her to have a glass of wine at dinner time.*
> - Use *let* (active only) to express permission.
>   *She let me have a go on her new mountain bike.*

> *permit, oblige, require,* and *forbid*
> - Use these verbs in impersonal or formal situations, e.g. in public announcements or on signs, and often in the passive form.
>   *Smoking is not permitted anywhere in this building.*
>   *Passengers are obliged to keep their luggage with them at all times.*

5 Match the beginnings and endings of the sentences.

1 I needn't have got there early ...

2 I didn't need to get there early ...

a ... because I knew the meeting wasn't until ten o'clock.

b ... because when I checked in, I was told that the plane was delayed.

3 I was told I didn't need to take my passport ...

4 I needn't have taken my passport ...

c ... so I left it at home.

d ... because you can use an identity card.

6 In pairs, make true sentences about recent experiences using *didn't need to* and *needn't have*.

7 Which sentences are wrong? Correct them.

1 They made him to tell the truth.

2 He was made to tell the truth.

3 My uncle lets me drive his car sometimes.

4 I was let to stay up late.

5 My parents never allowed to me to eat sweets.

8 In groups, make sentences about your childhood using *make, let,* and *allow*.

9 Rewrite the sentences to make impersonal statements using the words in *italics*.

1 You're not allowed to park on the yellow line.   *permit*

2 Passengers have to put their luggage in the overhead lockers.   *oblige*

3 You need a visa to go to most South American countries.   *require*

4 You mustn't take your mobile into the theatre.   *forbid*

10 In pairs, make five more true sentences using *permit, oblige, require,* and *forbid*.

Against the clock!

Set a time limit

11 Decide what you would say in these situations.

1 You're going out to dinner but your partner isn't ready and you're late.

2 You took your own picnic on a trip but lunch was provided.

3 At an interview, you are asked about your responsibilities in a previous job.

4 Your passport expires at the end of the month and you are going on holiday.

5 It wasn't necessary for you to keep your doctor's appointment because you felt better.

6 A new member of staff is asking about using the phone for personal reasons.

7 You are describing unpleasant things you were forced to do at school.

8 A visitor to your city is asking about driving and parking laws.

Speak out
Unusual communities

1 In groups of three, look at the photos. Where do you think the places are?

A

B

C

Think before you speak

- Use the language of obligation and necessity especially to describe rules and regulations.
- Experiment with different forms of *make*, *let*, and *allow*.
- Use your notes to remind you what to say. Try to use your own words.

2 **A** turn to *p.108*, **B** to *p.110*, **C** to *p.112*. Read about your place and make notes about your photo under the following headings:

- Location
- Population
- Language spoken
- Rules and regulations
- Anything else unusual

3 Tell the others about your place using the notes. Where would you like to live the most / least?

SUMMARY

Use *must / have got to*:

- to refer to your own future obligations.
  I must pay the phone bill.
- when the speaker has authority over the listener (parent / child, boss / employee).
  You must wash your hair, Sandra. It looks terrible.
- to make a recommendation.
  You've got to read this book. It's brilliant!

Use *mustn't*:

- to express a strong prohibition or warning.
  You mustn't play with that knife. It's very sharp.

Use *have to*:

- to talk about everyday obligations and responsibilities.
  I have to get up at 6.30 and take my son to school.

Use *don't have to*:

- when there is no obligation to do something.
  I don't have to go to work today because it's a national holiday.

Use *don't need to / needn't*:

- when something is unnecessary.
  You needn't water the plants. I did it yesterday.

Use *be + supposed to*:

- to express an obligation which is often ignored.
  You are supposed to wear a seatbelt in the back of the car but a lot of people don't bother.

07
POLITENESS PAYS

In this lesson

- Focus on making requests.
- Practise sounding more polite.
- Look at politeness in different cultures.

Speak for yourself

1 When was the last time someone was rude to you? What happened?

2 Read the joke. Do British people deserve a reputation for politeness?

An English woman was expecting a baby, but after nine and a half months nothing had happened so she went to the doctor. 'Well,' said the doctor, 'I am delighted to inform you that you are having twins.' 'But why are they so late?' asked the woman. 'Well,' the doctor explained, 'when one says, "After you", the other one replies, "No, I insist, after you." '

Reading

Words in context

1 Quickly read the text. Match cartoons **A** to **C** to the paragraphs.

A—

WHAT IS POLITE?

B—

C—

The British love to think of themselves as polite, and everyone knows how fond they are of their 'pleases' and 'thank yous'. Even the simplest transaction such as buying a train ticket requires at least seven or eight of these. Another sign of our good breeding is the queue. Casual visitors to Britain could be forgiven for thinking that queuing rather than cricket or football was the true national sport. Finally, of course, motorists generally stop at pedestrian crossings. _____ I think not.

Take forms of address. The average English person – unless he happens to work in a hotel or department store – would rather die than call a stranger 'Sir' or 'Madam'. _____ Our universal 'you' for everyone may appear more democratic, but it means that we are forced to seek out complicated ways to express politeness. I am all for reviving the use of 'thee' and 'thou'; 'you' would be reserved for strangers and professional relationships.

And of course, the English find touching and other shows of friendship truly terrifying. _____ Personally, I find the Latin habit of shaking hands or a friendly kiss quite charming. Try kissing the average English person, and they will either take two steps backwards in horror; or, if their escape is blocked, you will find your lips touching the back of their head. Now what could be ruder than that?

2 Where do sentences **a** to **c** go in the text?

a Have you noticed how the British hardly ever touch?

b Yet in most European countries this is the most basic of common courtesies.

c But does all this mean that the British should consider themselves more polite than their European neighbours?

3 Find words or expressions in the text which mean:

1 to like something or someone

2 when you buy or sell something

3 upbringing or manners

4 attractive or delightful

4 In pairs, decide how many different ways you have in your country ...
- of saying 'please' and 'thank you'.
- of saying 'you'.
- of showing friendship or greeting.

Listening
Making requests

1 In pairs, take turns to make a request or ask for permission, and agree or refuse.

You want to ...
- borrow a friend's car for the weekend.
- leave work early.
- ask a passer-by for directions to a chemist's.
- ask a stranger for the time.
- ask if someone can help you with a problem with your computer.
- tell someone in the cinema not to make so much noise.

2 Which different expressions did you use? Which are more polite?

3 Listen to eight conversations. Complete the chart.

Topic	Agrees (✓) or refuses (✗)
1	
2	
3	
4	
5	
6	
7	
8	

English in use
Being polite

1 Listen again. Complete the requests.

Requests	Replies
1 _____ your dictionary this weekend?	Sorry, normally I'd _____
2 _____ I smoke in here?	_____
3 _____ I open the window?	_____
4 _____ change for £5.00?	_____
5 _____ me a minute to look at this form.	_____
6 _____ I borrow your paper?	_____
7 _____ to that table in the shade?	_____
8 _____ continue your fascinating conversation after the lesson?	_____

2 Complete the replies and then check with the Tapescript on *p.114*.
Think of equivalent expressions in your language.

 3 Listen and copy the intonation.

    1 Which requests sound more polite?

    2 What's interesting about the teacher's request in Situation 8?

4 In pairs, practise the requests and replies.

Speak out
Asking nicely

Think before you speak

- Use as many different polite expressions as you can.
- Try to explain and persuade politely.
- Answer quickly and fluently using polite intonation.

Ask a colleague to give you a lift to the station. **start**	Ask permission to use someone's washing machine.	Order another bottle of wine in a restaurant.	Ask someone at the airport to take a piece of your luggage for you.
Ask permission to send a fax.			Ask a friend if you can borrow their car for the weekend.
Ask your boss for an extra week's holiday this summer.	Ask if the person in the next room can turn their radio down.	Ask your landlady if you can have a party in your flat.	Make an appointment to see a dentist as soon as possible.	Find out the prices of tickets for an important sporting or musical event.
Invite your friends for a meal.		Ask permission to change the channel in a public TV room.		
Ask if it's possible to move to a room which is less noisy.		Ask the manager of a hotel to explain your bill to you.		
Ask if it's OK to borrow some tools to repair something that's broken.	Ask the waiter for the bill.	Find out about sending a parcel to another country.		

Play in groups of four. Use a coin to move. Each time you land on a square you have five seconds to make your request. Nominate someone to reply. Explain your request and persuade the other person politely if they refuse.

1 square HEADS

TAILS 2 squares

In this lesson

- Extend your vocabulary to do with memories.
- Focus on vocabulary to do with the senses.
- Use *used to* and *would* to talk about early memories.

Speak for yourself

1 What are the five senses?
2 Which senses do you value most, and why?

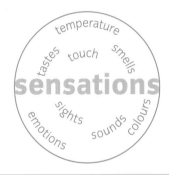

temperature
tastes touch smells
sensations
sights sounds colours
emotions

Reading

Words in context

1 Think back to your childhood. Remember one thing for each of the sensations in the circle.
2 Read about the actor Joss Ackland's childhood. Find examples of some of the sensations.

WHERE I GREW UP

Used to and *would*

Used to + base form and *would* + base form describe past habits and actions.

We used to / would play in the streets.

Only *used to* describes past states.

We used to live in a basement flat. NOT ~~We would live…~~

Find other examples in the text.

I was brought up almost solely by my mother. My father was an Irish journalist who was never around, but it wasn't until years later that I learned of his drinking. I was born below the ground, in a basement flat in North Kensington. One of my earliest memories is being pushed up the stairs of our flat. There was just one bedroom and the absolute bare essentials. We were very poor but poverty was accepted like life itself. I remember the railway bridge over Ladbroke Grove. Every time a train passed over I would imagine it crashing down on top of me. I spent little time indoors in our cramped flat. As we didn't have a garden I used to play in the streets. I remember the smell of black, dusty sacks of coal drawn by aged horses, but most of all I remember the fog. To be in the fog was an adventure where the imagination could stretch itself, allowing me to be anywhere in the world. Houses and streets would vanish and a lamp-post would faintly appear from the damp grey blanket which surrounded us and become a pirate ship. My first friend was my age, a black kid called Tino, and together we used to have tremendous adventures. When I look back to those early years the colours I see are browns and greys, but rich browns and greys nevertheless.

The Independent on Sunday

Vocabulary

remember, remind, forget

Memory words

1 to MEM _____
2 a final R _____
3 a MEM _____ occasion
4 a war MEM _____
5 an excellent MEM _____
6 an UNF _____ experience
7 a holiday S _____
8 a FOR _____ person

1 Listen to five different people, **a** to **e**. Which one ...?
1 talks about a romantic meeting place ☐
2 recounts a very early childhood memory ☐
3 describes an unpleasant school-time memory ☐
4 talks about people keeping in touch ☐
5 describes an important career choice ☐

2 Complete the sentences using an appropriate form of *remember, remind,* or *forget*.
1 Do you think you could _____ me to post this letter?
2 Don't _____ to buy a return ticket – it's much cheaper.
3 May I _____ you that we were here first. Join the back of the queue.
4 I'm sorry but I've _____ my wallet. Could you lend me a few pounds?
5 What money? I don't _____ borrowing any money from you!
6 _____ to get a ticket before you get on the train, otherwise you might have to pay a fine.

3 Complete the 'memory words' on the left. Use clues 1–8 below.
1 learn by heart
2 last chance to pay!
3 graduation day
4 to those who died
5 remember 200 telephone numbers
6 a bungee jump
7 a red bus from London, a sombrero from Spain
8 with a bad memory

Speak out
That takes me back

Visualize some early memories. Tell your partner/group about ...
- a childhood adventure or accident.
- an incident involving a favourite toy or pet.
- a place associated with your childhood.
- an important friendship.
- a family celebration.
- your grandparents.
- a first day at school.
- a holiday.

Think before you speak
- Talk about your memories related to the five senses.
- Use the vocabulary about memory you have studied.
- Use *would / used to* accurately to describe habits and states.

In this lesson

- Look at the organization of a story.
- Practise participating when listening to a story.
- Use extreme adjectives for emphasis and multi-word verbs to do with driving.

Speak for yourself

1 Imagine you are going to buy a brand new car. Which colour would you choose?

| silver | a pastel colour | black | green | grey | white | red | blue |

2 According to psychologist Conrad King, the colour of your car says more about your personality than the clothes you wear or the house you live in. Do you agree?

3 In pairs, match the colours above with the personality types in the chart.

Personality type	Colour choice
1 success-driven, ambitious	
2 outgoing, spontaneous, creative, easily bored	
3 stylish, a little self-important	
4 cold, distant, logical	
5 safe, cautious	
6 a team player, sociable, unimaginative	
7 class- and status-conscious	
8 depressive	

4 Compare with another pair. Then turn to *p.108* and check.

1 Would you stay with the colour choices you made?
2 Do you think there is any truth in Dr King's theories?
3 Do you think this survey would be valid in your country?

Listening
Understanding a story

1 Look at the photograph. What are they doing?

2 Listen to Julian's story. Write 'true' or 'false'.

Part 1

1 The story happened while Julian was at university.
2 He and his friend had very little money left.
3 They got a very good lift all the way from Germany to the centre of France.
4 The village was convenient for passing traffic.
5 They tried to hitch from the middle of the village.

Part 2

6 The driver wanted someone to talk to.
7 Julian was nervous.
8 The driver fell asleep.
9 They hit a tree.
10 Tony was badly hurt.

Story chart

→ Stage 1 ☐
General background / introduction

→ Stage 2 ☐
Leading into the main story

→ Stage 3 ☐
The main part of the story

→ Stage 4 ☐
What happened in the end

→ Stage 5 ☐
Feelings about the story now

3 The story you have just heard follows a typical pattern. When you are listening to a story, it helps if you can recognize this pattern.

1 Match the key phrases **a** to **e** to the five stages in the chart.

a Anyway, we had been down to Greece and were making our way back, and had almost run out of money when ...

b I'll never forget something that happened to me when I went hitch-hiking one summer ...

c It's put me off hitch-hiking for ever, though ...

d Anyway, about ten o'clock that evening the inevitable happened, we were coming up to a roundabout and he fell asleep just for a second ...

e After breakfast he dropped us off at the main road and we said goodbye ...

2 Check with the Tapescript on *p.114*. Mark the five stages.

3 Which tenses does he tend to use for each part of the story?

Vocabulary
Multi-word verbs

1 Complete the multi-word verbs.

1 You'd better _____ **down**. The roads are icy.

2 Do you think you could _____ **up** the children from school?

3 You should always _____ **way** to traffic coming from the right.

4 That was close! We almost _____ **over** that cat.

5 I can _____ you **off** at the station on my way to work.

6 Oh dear. I think that police car wants us to _____ **over**.

7 We've almost _____ **out of** petrol. I hope we find a garage.

Extreme adjectives

When people tell entertaining stories they often exaggerate.

I was scared – I was absolutely terrified.

We modify standard adjectives with *very*, but extreme adjectives with *absolutely*.

very angry – absolutely furious

Really can modify standard and extreme adjectives.

When we want to emphasize or exaggerate we repeat the standard adjective, and then use emphatic stress with a falling intonation on the extreme adjective.

Tired? He was exhausted.

2 Write standard adjectives for each extreme adjective. *furious – angry*

furious	gorgeous	horrified	filthy
fascinating	wonderful	hideous	terrifying
huge	brilliant	exhausted	awful
tiny	delighted	ghastly	delicious

3 ▣2 Listen and mark the stress.

Sue   How **awful**! You must have been really **scared** ...

Julian   **Scared**! I was **absolutely terrified**! I was shaking like a leaf.

4 Listen again, and copy the intonation.

5 In pairs, practise responding with an extreme adjective.

1 That film was really bad, wasn't it?   *Bad? It was absolutely awful.*

2 You look very tired.

3 Were you frightened when you saw the burglar?

4 The hotel we stayed in was rather dirty.

5 We were angry when we saw the phone bill.

English in use
Commenting

When people tell stories, they expect to do most of the talking. However, they also expect listeners to participate by making short comments or asking questions. The purpose of these is usually to:

- get more information.
- show sympathy/concern.
- show surprise.

They help the story develop.

 1 Listen and complete the short comments by the listeners.

1 What, _____ ?

2 Oh _____ .

3 That was _____ .

4 Really? _____ ?

5 So _____ ?

6 How _____ !

A good way to lead from one story to another is to comment and then to say that the story you have just heard reminds you of something else.

I'm not surprised! … You know, this reminds me of something that happened a few years ago …

How awful! … It's just like something that happened to me last year …

2 In pairs, comment and lead into another similar story.

1 I locked myself out of my flat last night.

2 I took the wrong train the other day.

3 When I wanted to pay I realized I didn't have enough money.

4 What am I going to do? I've lost the watch my grandmother gave me.

Speak out
It happened to me

1 In pairs, look at the list and choose a topic you want to tell a story about. Make a few notes.

- a day to remember
- a concert or sporting event
- an incident from my school days
- getting lost
- a frightening experience
- a lucky escape
- moving house

2 In groups, each pair should talk for one minute. The others should make comments or ask questions.

Think before you speak

- Try to follow the five stages for telling a story.
- When you are listening, make sure that you comment on what is said and ask questions to move the story on.
- Use multi-word verbs and extreme adjectives.
- Remember to use the correct intonation with extreme adjectives.
- Try to lead into your own story.

10
DRIVING PASSIONS

In this lesson

- Revise and extend uses of past narrative tenses.
- Extend your driving vocabulary.
- Practise skim-reading.
- Practise telling stories.

Speak for yourself

1 How good a driver do you think you are/would be?

2 In pairs, put these words/phrases into the spidergram below.

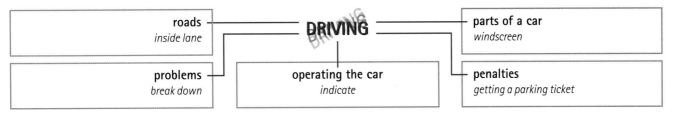

get a puncture	spare tyre	be banned from (driving)
flash your lights	boot	be charged with (drink-driving)
accelerate	crash into	stuck in a traffic jam
be fined (£100)	hard shoulder	be prosecuted for (speeding)
seat belt	airbag	overtake
brake	run out of petrol	roundabout
lay-by	exit	change gear

roads
inside lane

DRIVING

parts of a car
windscreen

problems
break down

operating the car
indicate

penalties
getting a parking ticket

Text A

Two motorway patrol officers on the M25 motorway around London were sitting in a lay-by next to the inside lane when a car in the outside lane suddenly stopped opposite them. 'We're lost,' shouted driver Peter Cray across the two lanes, as the cars which were following braked and began crashing into each other. Cray was charged with parking on a motorway and was banned from driving for a year.

Text B

A motorist sped past a carload of policemen at 100 mph while he was shaving with an electric razor. The 22-year-old salesman came up behind the officers on the M40 motorway as they were travelling to a conference. The salesman flashed his lights at the unmarked car, and then overtook it on the inside lane. As he shot past, one of the officers showed him his identity card through the window so the young man took the next exit from the motorway. However, he was caught, banned from driving for seven months, and fined £500.

Reading
Skimming texts

1 Skim-read these true stories. Match them to pictures 1 to 4.

2 Are older drivers safer than younger drivers?

1 —

2 —

3 —

4 —

Text C

In 1993, a pensioner was prosecuted by the police. He had caused a 25-mile traffic jam behind him because he had been driving so slowly!

Text D

At the age of 84, Rosie Milvain became the oldest person ever to have passed the driving test. In actual fact she had already been driving for 67 years, but had been forced to take one after being fined for dangerous driving. Unfortunately, the day after Rosie made history, her brand new car was stolen while she was doing her shopping. Naturally she reported the theft to the police. However, when the police finally discovered the car a few hours later it had not been stolen at all. She had forgotten that she had left it in a nearby car park.

Tony Bosworth

Past narrative forms

Grammar revisited

1 Look at Texts **A** and **B** again. Find examples of the past simple and the past continuous.

2 Discuss when we use the different forms. Check your answers in the Summary on *p.31*.

3 Look at the pictures below. In pairs, tell the story.

MY BROTHER!

Grammar plus

> **The past perfect simple**
>
> **Form**
>
> subject + *had* + past participle
>   He **had** already **eaten** something.
>
> **Use**
>
> • to describe a completed action which happened in the 'past before the past'.
>   *When I arrived at the party Sarah had already left.*

4 Look at the timeline below. Which tenses are used and why?

5 Find other examples of the past perfect simple and continuous in Text **D**. Illustrate the meanings on timelines.

> **The past perfect continuous**
>
> **Form**
>
> subject + *had been* + present participle
>   He **had been living** there all his life.
>
> **Use**
>
> • to describe a longer activity leading up to a point in the past.
>   *I had been waiting outside the cinema for an hour when Peter finally arrived.*
>
> • to describe a repeated action leading up to a point in the past.
>   *She had been sending him letters for seven years.*

Against the clock!

Set a time limit

6 In pairs, look at these extracts from letters. Who do you think received them?

7 Complete the extracts. Use the verbs in brackets.

1 An invisible car _____ (come) out of nowhere, hit my car, and _____ (disappear).

2 I _____ (knock) the man over. He admitted that it was his fault as he _____ (be knocked over) before.

3 I _____ (shop) for plants all day and I was on my way home. As I _____ (reach) a junction, a tree suddenly _____ (block) my view, and I _____ (not see) the other car.

4 I _____ (arrive) home, drove into the wrong garage, and _____ (crash) into a car I don't have.

5 I _____ (notice) a sad-faced, slow-moving old gentleman as he _____ (land) on the bonnet of my car.

6 I realized that I _____ (forget) to take off the anti-theft lock and I had only travelled about 20 metres when I _____ (hit) a parked car.

7 I _____ (do) 28 mph. I am sure of this, as I _____ (look) at the speedometer when I hit him.

8 The driver _____ (sneeze) and his false teeth _____ (fall out). While he _____ (look for) them he crashed into another car.

Tony Bosworth

The pensioner was **prosecuted**. He **had caused** a 25-mile traffic jam because he **had been driving** so slowly.

Past ————×———————×————————×———————— Now
     had been driving   *had caused*   *prosecuted*

Speak out
A driving story

In groups, tell each other a driving story from your personal experience. Take it in turns to choose a topic. When you have finished one topic, move on to another.

Think before you speak

- Use a variety of narrative tenses accurately to tell your story.
- Include at least five new words or phrases about driving.
- Use *then*, *after*, *afterwards*, and *after that* correctly.

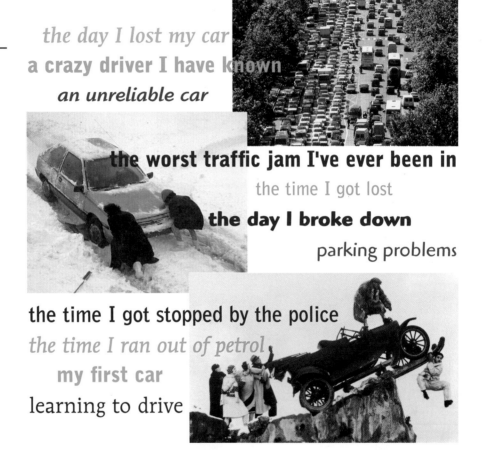

the day I lost my car

a crazy driver I have known

an unreliable car

the worst traffic jam I've ever been in

the time I got lost

the day I broke down

parking problems

the time I got stopped by the police

the time I ran out of petrol

my first car

learning to drive

SUMMARY

Use the past simple:

- to express a finished single action in the past when the time is either stated or implied.
  I bought my car two years ago.
- to describe a series of completed actions.
  They ate lunch, put the suitcases in the boot, and set off.
- for repeated actions over a period of time.
  I always went swimming on Saturday mornings when I was a teenager.

Use the past continuous:

- for descriptions in the past.
  It was snowing heavily and everyone was hurrying home.

- to describe an interrupted action in the past.
  He was running for the bus when he slipped and fell.
- to describe an interrupted action which may or may not have continued.
  When we arrived they were in the middle of painting the dining-room ceiling.

Then/after that, after, and afterwards

Complete these sentences using *then/after that*, *after*, or *afterwards*.

1 _____ we had had dinner we went to the pub.

2 First we had dinner and _____ we went to the pub.

3 We had dinner and _____ we went to the pub.

- *after* is not usually used alone as an adverb.
  I wrote a letter and then/after that/afterwards I went to the meeting. NOT ~~after I went to the meeting~~.

11 HIGHLY RECOMMENDED

In this lesson
- Look at making recommendations.
- Practise talking about things you enjoyed seeing, reading, or visiting.
- Extend your use of adjectives to describe things precisely.

Speak for yourself

1 Tell a partner quickly about ...
- some music you like.
- a meal you really enjoyed.
- the last book you read.

2 Look at a survey of British tastes. How similar are they to your own tastes?

UK tastes	music		take-away food	books	
	41% pop	7% jazz	1 curry	1 thrillers and detective stories	4 science fiction
	23% rock	5% easy listening	2 fish and chips	2 adventure stories	5 contemporary fiction
	11% soul / reggae	2% country / folk	3 Chinese	3 romances	6 humorous books
	11% classical				

3 Do you think there is such a thing as 'national taste'? Could you describe tastes in your own country?

Vocabulary

Taste

1 How do we use these words / phrases? Give examples.

tasteful	tasty	tasteless	in bad taste

2 **Against the clock!** In pairs, in two minutes ...
1. Match the opposites of the food and drink adjectives on the left.
2. Think of as many foods / drinks as you can for each.

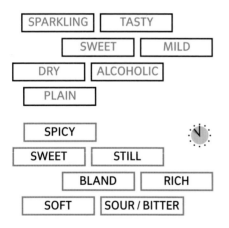

SPARKLING   TASTY
SWEET   MILD
DRY   ALCOHOLIC
PLAIN

SPICY
SWEET   STILL
BLAND   RICH
SOFT   SOUR / BITTER

3 Match the definitions with the adjectives in **bold** in sentences 1 to 10.

average	very impressive	fascinating
small and cosy	fashionable	not interesting
exciting	easy to guess what's going to happen	
long and boring	sets a particular scene or mood	

1 *The state-of-the-art special effects in his latest film are* **stunning**.

2 **The plot was really gripping – I couldn't put it down.**

3 We were rather disappointed – the food was **uninspiring** to say the least.

4 *The descriptions are really* **atmospheric** *– I felt as though I was there.*

5 It was so **predictable** – I knew what was going to happen after the first few pages.

6 His work is terribly **mediocre** – it did nothing for me at all.

7 *The concert went on for hours and the music was very* **tedious**.

8 I enjoyed the play – the characters were **intriguing** and the script well-written.

9 *The jazz bar is small and friendly – an* **intimate** *atmosphere.*

10 The Rock Club is full of **trendy** people wearing the latest fashions.

Reading
Time out

1 How often do you read newspaper or magazine reviews to help you decide what to do? Do you think they are reliable?

2 Read the three reviews. Rate them as follows:

★★★★ highly recommended   ★★ mediocre

★★★ good   ★ a waste of time

Mechanics
by Seamus O'Riordan

Set on both sides of the Atlantic in the 1980s, this 'IRA against FBI' story is yet another tasteless example of the 'crazy terrorist kills cop's best friend' genre of thriller. Predictable and mediocre, the author fills out its 600 pages with tedious details of weapons and graphic descriptions of violence, but wastes no time on the less than gripping plot. If you want an unexciting airport 'read', this is for you.

Seattle Piano Bar

Not the atmospheric jazz cellar we were expecting, but instead, a décor of dazzling chrome and unforgiving neon lights, and a super-trendy clientele. However, light, cool jazz piano, and delicious cocktails softened the atmosphere. The menu looked good, but the results were dull and uninspiring. We ordered seafood crepes, which turned out to be cold and rubbery. So-so service, too, from staff you feel were chosen for good looks alone. Perhaps we weren't trendy enough.

Ivy Giorgevski
at the Alma Theatre Club

Born of a Polish mother and Jamaican father, Ivy Giorgevski is simply stunning. She caressed us with an intriguing menu ranging from rhythmic jazz through to country rock and opera. Her mellow voice, reminiscent of Ella Fitzgerald, lacked the range for a couple of the more operatic pieces, but nevertheless has real virtuoso quality, and the intimate venue was perfect for her style. Just three more nights, so hurry along.

3 Find expressions in each text to show how strongly the reviewer feels.

Listening
Highly recommended

1 Listen to three conversations. Make notes in Column 1 of the chart.

Column 1	Column 2
Film	Why they recommend it
Title *The Commitments*	
Setting	
Main characters	
Story	
Book	
Title *Captain Corelli's Mandolin*	
Setting	
Main characters	
Story	
Restaurant	
Name *Vijay's*	
Location	
Kind of restaurant	

2 Listen again. Complete Column 2.

3 Would you enjoy the film, the book, or the restaurant? Why/why not?

English in use
Making recommendations

1 Look at stages 1 to 4 for 'Making recommendations' below. Match a title from the box to each stage.

Providing details	Describing the experience
Making the recommendation	Leading into a recommendation

1 _____

Say where it is, how you heard about it, why you went, who with, etc.

It's on at the Palace Theatre.
(Dave) told me about it. / I read about it in the paper.
We went for my birthday.

2 _____

Say what it's about, who's in it / main characters (if it's a book, film, etc.)

It's set in Dublin, and it's about a group of young people who …

What's involved (if it's a concert, art exhibition, etc.), or what it's like (if it's a restaurant, club, etc.).

It's Kappur's latest exhibition that's just come from New York.
It doesn't look much from the outside but the food's really tasty.

3 _____

Use adjectives to describe it in detail.

It was (absolutely) stunning / gripping.
It was (rather) predictable / mediocre / uninspiring.
It isn't / doesn't sound like my sort of thing.
The best bit was … / worst thing was …

4 _____

Say whether you think it's worth seeing / visiting / doing.

You (really) should see it / go there / try it.
You must read it for yourself.
I wouldn't bother if I were you.

Use exaggerated intonation to show that you were enthusiastic / unimpressed.

 2 Listen and copy the intonation.

Speak out
Personal reviews

Think before you speak

- Use the language of making recommendations to persuade the others of your point of view.
- Use the right vocabulary to give your opinions accurately.
- Use intonation to express clearly how you feel.

1 In groups, talk about something you would highly recommend or not recommend from your recent experience. Choose one of the following or something of your own.

BOOK	FILM	EXHIBITION	FOOD	CD

2 In the same groups, agree on one thing only from each of the above categories to have on a desert island.

12
SAME BUT DIFFERENT

In this lesson

- Look at 'false friends' and other easily confused words.
- Use expressions with the key word *mind*.
- Practise talking about an embarrassing experience.

Speak for yourself

Look at these notices in 'English' from around the world. What did they really mean to say?

1 — **FUR COATS**
MADE FOR LADIES
FROM THEIR OWN SKIN

In the window of a Swedish shop selling fur coats

2 — Drive sideways

Road sign in Japan

3 — *We take your bags and send them in all directions.*

Copenhagen airline ticket office

4 — HERE SPEECHING ENGLISH

Shop in Majorca

5 — Please do not feed the animals. If you have any suitable food, give it to the guard on duty.

At a Budapest zoo

Reading

Words in context

1 Read the beginning of the story about Tricia's experience in Madrid. In pairs, put the rest of the text in the right order.

2 Are there any words in your language that foreigners often have problems with?

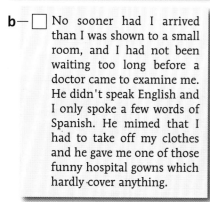

A few years ago I went on holiday to Spain but unfortunately, after two days in Madrid, I started to get terrible back pain. I was in such agony that I went to the local hospital for an examination.

a — ☐ I was beginning to wonder what had happened to him when he suddenly reappeared, this time with a group of medical students, and again asked the same question in Spanish. Now I was feeling upset, and shouted in English, 'Yes I am extremely embarrassed. I think you would mind too if you had to talk to a crowd of strangers with almost no clothes on.' Then a female doctor in the group gently held my arm and whispered in perfect English, 'I think I see the problem.'

b — ☐ No sooner had I arrived than I was shown to a small room, and I had not been waiting too long before a doctor came to examine me. He didn't speak English and I only spoke a few words of Spanish. He mimed that I had to take off my clothes and he gave me one of those funny hospital gowns which hardly cover anything.

c — ☐ You see, my colleague wants to take a photograph of your back – an X-ray – so he wants to know if you are expecting a baby. You see, *embarazada* means pregnant in Spanish.' No sooner had she told me this than I realized the cause of the misunderstanding. We all had a laugh, although I must admit that I felt rather stupid as well.

d — ☐ He then asked me in Spanish if I was embarrassed. '*Si, un poco* (Yes, a little)', I replied, blushing deeply. You see, not only did I feel embarrassed at taking off my clothes in front of a stranger but also this particular stranger was an extremely handsome man. He looked at me as though I was out of my mind and then disappeared down the corridor.

Vocabulary
False friends

1 Use a dictionary. Choose the correct word.

  1 That child is very badly **educated** / **behaved**; he keeps sticking his tongue out.

  2 I can't find that book I borrowed from the **library** / **bookshop**.

  3 There's a wonderful **exposition** / **exhibition** at the Louvre.

  4 I can't eat ice-cream because I've got very **sensitive** / **sensible** teeth.

  5 'Where's your brother **at the moment** / **actually**?' 'He's in Brussels.'

  6 Thanks for the invitation; I'll write it in my **diary** / **agenda** straight away.

  7 That newspaper is just government **advertising** / **propaganda**.

  8 You're really putting on weight; you should go on a **regime** / **diet**.

 2 **Against the clock!** In teams, work out the meanings of these easily confused words in five minutes.

1 shade / shadow	6	unhelpful / helpless
2 recipe / receipt	7	fantasy / imagination
3 beach / shore	8	embarrassed / ashamed
4 opportunity / possibility	9	worthless / priceless
5 warehouse / department store	10	middle ages / middle-aged

Key word
mind

Make up your mind!

I don't mind

Mind out!

out of my mind

MIND

a lot on my mind

Mind you

Never mind

speak my mind

1 Match sentences 1 to 8 with responses **a** to **h**.

  1 Do you mind if I bring a friend?

  2 Which one? I can't make up my mind.

  3 She must be out of her mind.

  4 He's got a lot on his mind.

  5 Can I speak my mind?

  6 Mind you, she is eighteen, you know.

  7 It's broken. Never mind.

  8 Mind your head.

  a I thought he was looking worried.

  b Yes, it's a crazy thing to do!

  c It depends who it is.

  d Sorry, I'll buy you another one.

  e What did you say? Ouch!

  f I still think she's too young.

  g I think the first one suits you best.

  h Yes, it's important to be frank.

 2 Listen and respond using an expression with *mind*.

Speak out
Things we'd rather forget

Choose one of the pictures. Imagine you are the main character. Tell the story. Add as much detail as you can.

Think **before you speak**

- Use Tricia's story as a model: set the scene, describe what happened, describe the result.
- Use any new vocabulary from the lesson correctly.
- Include expressions with *mind*.

13
GETTING THROUGH

In this lesson

- Practise the language and skills of telephoning.
- Look at different levels of formality.
- Extend your knowledge of multi-word verbs for telephoning.

Speak for yourself

1 In Britain, when people answer the phone at home they often say their number, or simply 'Hello'. What happens in your country?

2 Listen and write the four phone numbers.

3 Listen again. Copy the intonation.
   1 How does the speaker divide each number up?
   2 What does the speaker's voice do at the end of each group of numbers?
   3 Is this the same or different in your country?

4 In pairs, **A** turn to *p.108*, **B** to *p.111*. Complete the phone numbers.

Reading
Understanding tone

1 Ask a partner.
   1 In which situations do you often find it difficult to get through to people on the phone, e.g. railway stations?
   2 When you finally speak to someone, how helpful / polite are they?

2 Read **Part 1** of the text.
   1 Is Bryson's experience similar to your own?
   2 How do you think Bryson wants us to react to his story, e.g. be angry on his behalf, smile, feel sorry for him ...? Underline examples in the text to justify your answers.

Part 1

Bill Bryson, an American writer and journalist, lived in Britain for many years before moving back to the United States. He talks about his experience of telephoning a US government office for some information.

The other day I had an experience so surprising and unexpected that it made me spill a drink down my shirt. What caused this was that I called a faceless government bureaucracy – specifically, the US Social Security Administration – and someone answered the phone. I was expecting to hear a recorded voice tell me, 'All our agents are busy, so please hold while we play you some *irritating* music interrupted at 15-second intervals by a recorded voice telling you all our agents are busy, so please hold while we play you some irritating music ...' and so on until teatime.

So imagine my surprise when, after just 270 rings, a real person came on the line. He asked me some of my personal details, to determine the best way he could make this a frustrating experience for me, then said, 'Excuse me, Bill, I have to put you on hold for a minute.'

irritating annoying

3 Read **Part 2.**

1 For Bryson, what is a key difference between British and US society?

2 How have his feelings about the informality of US society changed?

Part 2

Did you catch that? He called me 'Bill'. Not 'Mr Bryson'. Not 'Sir'. Not 'Oh *Mighty* Taxpayer'. But 'Bill'. Two years ago I would have regarded this as a *gross impertinence*, but now I find I've rather grown to like it. There are certain times when the informality and familiarity of American life strain my patience – when a waiter tells me his name is Bob and he is going to be my server for this evening, I still have an urge to say, 'I just want a cheeseburger, Bob. I'm not looking for a relationship.' – but mostly I have come to like it.

There is a genuine, unselfconscious, universal assumption that no person is better than any other. I think that's great. My dustman calls me Bill. My doctor calls me Bill. My children's headteacher calls me Bill. I think that's as it should be. In England, I used the same accountant for a decade and our relations were always very friendly but businesslike. She never called me anything but Mr Bryson and I never called her anything but Mrs Creswick. When I moved to America, I phoned an accountant for an appointment. When I came to his office, his first words to me were, 'Ah, Bill, I'm glad you could make it.' We were *pals* already, you see.

The Mail on Sunday

mighty powerful, important
gross impertinence very disrespectful behaviour
pals friends

4 Which of these two cultures is closer to your own? In your country, would you expect to be on first name terms in a professional context?

Vocabulary
Multi-word verbs

1 Complete the multi-word verbs.

1 She's not in her office but if you'd like to _____ **on** a minute I'll find her.

2 His line's free now, caller. I'm just _____ you **through**.

3 I can hardly hear you, Melanie. Can you _____ **up**?

4 Hello, Janet, hello – the line has gone dead. I think we've been _____ **off**.

5 Oh no, the number's still engaged. I've been trying to _____ **through** all day.

6 There is no news yet, but I promise I'll _____ you **up** as soon as I know.

7 If you don't know the number try _____ it **up** in the phone book.

8 Sorry dad, but my taxi is waiting outside. I've got to _____ **up**.

9 Could you tell her I'll _____ **back** later.

10 If the phone rings, please don't _____ it **up**. I'm expecting a fax.

2 In groups, decide what you would say in the following telephone situations. Use the multi-word verbs above.

1 — You are talking to your friend Maria, but you can hardly hear her voice.

2 — You are talking on the phone when suddenly the line goes dead.

3 — Someone has asked you to take a message but you haven't got a pen.

4 — You get a call for a colleague but she is out. Suggest the caller tries again in an hour.

5 — You want to transfer a call. Explain to the caller that you are going to try and connect them to another department.

6 — You are trying to organize a theatre visit for a group of friends. Explain that you have been trying to phone the theatre all day without success. The line is always busy.

7 — A friend has rung to ask for the number of a hotel you stayed in. Ask them to wait while you find the number.

8 — You are about to go out to the cinema when the telephone rings. Tell your friend not to answer it. Say the caller can leave a message.

Listening
Dealing with different callers

 1 Put Conversation 1 in the correct order. Listen and check.

 2 Listen to Conversation 2. Complete the expressions.

Conversation 1

a ☐1 **Karen** Mr Blakemore's office, Karen speaking.

b ☐ **Rona** Certainly, thank you very much ...

c ☐ **Rona** Yes, my name's Rona Cash, I'm a reporter from the Essex Messenger.

d ☐ **Rona** Well, it's regarding the new shopping centre; I was wondering if he could discuss some questions about the plans.

e ☐ **Karen** Well, I'm not quite sure, but if you'd like to give me your details I'll make sure he calls you back.

f ☐ **Rona** Good morning, could I speak to Mr Blakemore, please?

g ☐ **Karen** ... Hello, Miss Cash. I'm afraid he's going to be busy all morning.

h ☐ **Karen** If you'd like to hold the line for a moment I'll see if he's available ...

i ☐ **Karen** I see, and can I ask what it's in connection with?

j ☐ **Rona** OK, when would be a good time for me to call again?

k ☐ **Karen** May I ask who's calling?

Conversation 2

1 Who's _____ ?

2 _____ Paul Walsh _____ .

3 So, what _____ ?

4 Is she _____ ?

5 _____ a minute.

6 I'll see if _____ .

7 She's _____ with a client.

8 _____ a message?

9 _____ the cover design.

10 I'll get _____ she's free.

11 _____ mobile.

12 Right, _____ .

English in use
Levels of formality

1 Find phrases from Conversations 1 and 2.

How do people ...?	
• introduce themselves	• ask the caller to wait
• ask who is calling	• say someone is busy
• ask the reason for the call	• say someone will return the call

2 Write **less formal** equivalents   ... and **more formal**

1 in connection with/regarding	6 Hi!
2 available	7 hang on
3 certainly	8 tied up
4 I'm afraid	9 sort out
5 to telephone/to call	10 fire away

Think before you speak

- Adjust your level of formality to the type of conversation.
- Use as many multi-word verbs and telephone expressions as you can.
- Use the correct intonation for phone numbers.

Speak out
Telephoning

A turn to *p.108*, **B** to *p.111*. Roleplay two phone conversations.

In this lesson

- Revise and extend ways of expressing the future.
- Focus on (un)*likely to* and *bound to* to express probability.
- Practise talking about possible future events.

Speak for yourself

1 What different ways do you know of predicting the future, e.g. palm reading, horoscopes, etc.? Do you believe in any of them?

2 Read about Nostradamus. Do you believe he could see into the future?

3 Which of the predictions 'Until 2016' do you think will happen?

Nostradamus was a 16th century *clairvoyant* and astrologer, who was also a doctor of medicine. After his wife and children died of the plague he began to write his twelve volumes of prophecies, *The Centuries*, covering thousands of years into the future. The verses are written in 16th century French, and are expressed in symbolic language. Here are some of his predictions as collected and interpreted by Peter Lorie:

The 20th century	Until 2016
• political and economic chaos throughout the 20th century • the rise of Hitler and the Gulf War • the growth of the Japanese nation and its economic power • the birth of Communism in Russia, and the end of the Cold War • the coming of a great plague which many people link to AIDS • the divorce of Charles and Diana • holes in the ozone layer	• an upheaval in the government of China • the emergence of a single world leader • a woman president of the USA • the political survival of the new Germany after reunification • the election of a French Pope • political changes and the end of secret bank accounts in Switzerland • a series of natural disasters

clairvoyant someone who can see into the future

Listening
Everyday situations

 1 Listen to five short extracts, **a** to **e**. Which ...?

1 involves making decisions ☐   4 involves predictions ☐
2 has someone asking for information ☐   5 involves an invitation ☐
3 is a warning ☐

2 Listen again. Choose **a**, **b**, or **c**.

1 Martin's father
  a is going to break his son's neck.   b approves of his son's behaviour.
  c seriously worries about his son's safety.

2 Jan is
  a disappointed.   b relieved.   c looking forward to the weekend.

3 Melanie
  a isn't hungry.   b is popular.   c is insensitive to the others.

4 The clerk
  a thinks the man will catch the train.   b wants to go to Cambridge.
  c doesn't think the man will catch the train.

5 The weather this weekend
  a will be mixed.   b will be mostly sunny.   c will be terrible.

Ways of expressing the future

Grammar revisited

1 🔘2 Listen and complete sentences 1 to 6.

1 _____ break your neck.
2 _____ a colleague this weekend.
3 _____ the steak with the Roquefort sauce.
4 _____ the steak.
5 The next one _____ in two minutes.
6 The bad weather _____ on Sunday morning.

2 With a partner, decide why these different ways of expressing the future are used. Check your answers using the Summary on *p.42.*

3 In pairs, decide what you would say in the following situations.

1 Someone asks you about your plans for next weekend.
2 It's raining hard but your friend insists on cycling home.
3 You see an elderly person reaching for something high on a supermarket shelf.
4 A friend suggests going to the beach but it is cloudy.
5 Members of your family want to know more about what you are doing for the summer holiday.
6 Someone asks you about your arrangements for a business trip.

Grammar plus

4 🔘3 Listen and complete the answerphone messages.

1
> Gwen, hi, it's Michael here. I'm just ringing to say that ¹_____ tomorrow evening – that's Friday – at Heathrow, at around 6.30. The flight's ²_____ delayed 'cos of the weather this end, but even so, expect to see me ³_____. Don't bother to make anything, will you, 'cos ⁴_____ on the plane. Anyway, I'm really ⁵_____ seeing you. Till tomorrow then. Bye.

2
> It's Tessa from the garage here. The 'child seat' you ordered is ⁶_____ to arrive later on this morning. Joe ⁷_____ it after lunch and it ⁸_____ him too long. I'd say it's ⁹_____ to be ready by round about three; ¹⁰_____ it by then. Perhaps we'd better say ¹¹_____, though, just to be safe.

5 Which verb forms are used and why?

6 🔘4 Listen and note the contractions. Copy the intonation.

The future continuous

Form

subject + *will be* + present participle
*I **will be leaving** soon.*

Use

- to talk about an action in progress at / around a point in the future.
  This time tomorrow, I will be sitting in the plane.
- for polite enquiries.
  Will you be staying for dinner?
- to talk about future events which are fixed or expected to happen in the normal course of things.
  Next term Gemma will be running yoga classes at the same time every week.

The future perfect

Form

subject + *will have* + past participle
*He **will have finished** soon.*

Use

- to talk about something that will be completed / achieved before a point in the future.
  I will have finished this report by the end of the day.

Adjectival phrases

- *be bound to* for something certain / inevitable.
  It's (absolutely) bound to rain if we take a picnic.
- *be (highly) (un)likely to* if something is (im)probable.
  They are likely to be late because of the traffic.
- *be due to* if something is expected.
  She's due to arrive on the 6.15 train.

🕐 Against the clock!

Set a time limit _____

7 Make some notes about yourself and your future using the chart.

	you	family	friends	colleagues	your country
next year					
this year					
this week					
today					

8 In pairs, compare charts and your futures.

Replying to questions

Often when we reply to questions about the future we use *hope* and *think*.

- Do you think you'll be living with your parents this time next year?
  I think so / I don't think so.
- Will they be able to clone human beings in the future?
  I hope so / I hope not.

Speak out
Future news

Effective reading
We often scan-read newspapers to find things which interest us.
- Look at the headlines to help you predict what the stories might be about.
- Scan each story quickly to see if you are interested in it.

1 Scan through the eight news stories quickly. Match them to the headlines. Which three sound the most interesting to you?

HISTORIC VICTORY FOR MOHANDAS ☐   *Life on Mars* ☐

Protest continues ☐   ***Save our SERVE!*** ☐

IN YOUR OWN IMAGE ☐   Death to the dollar ☐

AIDS breakthrough ☐   **A single language** ☐

A—Even though prices start at $500,000, there is still a year's waiting list at the New York Organ Clinic, which is now able to replace organs to order from animal and human tissue. The service includes genetic enhancement, enabling patients to benefit from improved-quality organs. It is hoped that this service will be available in Europe within a couple of years.

B—Top tennis players protested last night against the introduction of a single serve in professional matches. This is an attempt to end the 'power serve' which has dominated tennis for so many years.

C—The United World Nations last night ratified the Global Currency Agreement. The new currency (the Glocu) will come into effect worldwide in February next year. It is hoped that the move will do much to stabilize ailing economies across the globe.

D—The European Union has decided to adopt English as its official language. From January 1st next year all business will have to be conducted in English. The vote was closely contested, English beating Spanish by a narrow margin.

E—Loretta Mohandas has won 76% of the vote to become the USA's first black woman president. A few years ago people would have said a black woman president in the White House was an impossibility.

F—Shield, the new vaccine which provides 100% protection against the Aids virus, will be available to the public within the next year.

G—Colonists living in the Columbus Biosphere have celebrated the first anniversary of living on Mars with a birthday party for James Ortega, the first child to be born on the planet.

H—Language teachers are continuing their strike in protest against the 'lingua' computer chip implant which allows students to learn a new language effortlessly. Teachers say they are fighting for their jobs and their survival.

Think before you speak
- Use appropriate forms for expressing the future as accurately as you can.
- Use *likely to* and *bound to* to express probability.
- Use contractions and weak forms where appropriate.

2 In groups, decide how probable the stories are. Agree together, and rank them in order of how likely they are to happen (1=likely, 8=highly unlikely). Give reasons.

SUMMARY

Use the present continuous
- to talk about fixed personal arrangements.
  I'm meeting Chris at 8.00 on Wednesday evening.

Use *going to*
- to express future intentions.
  I'm going to work really hard next week.
- to make predictions based on present evidence.
  Look at those clouds. I think it's going to rain.

Use *will*
- to state a future fact.
  I will be 35 in the year 2020.
- to make a prediction based on your knowledge or opinion.
  I think the economic situation will start to improve soon.
- to express a promise, an offer, or a decision.
  I'll help you with that bag. It looks heavy.

Use the present simple
- for regular time-tabled events.
  My train leaves at 8.30 on Saturday.

15 DRESS FOR SUCCESS

In this lesson
- Focus on how to do well in interviews.
- Practise sounding enthusiastic and confident.
- Use expressions with the key word *look*.

Speak for yourself

Rate your opinion for each statement. Explain to a partner.

| strongly agree | 1 | 2 | 3 | 4 | 5 | strongly disagree |

- ☐ People worry too much about how they look.
- ☐ Uniforms are a good idea.
- ☐ I would have confidence in a doctor who was wearing an old pair of jeans.
- ☐ My first impression of someone is nearly always correct.
- ☐ People express their character through the clothes they wear.

A —

Listening
Going for an interview

1 You're going to listen to Joanna King giving advice to a group of job-seekers. Look at the cartoons. Predict what she's going to say.

2 🔊1 Listen and make notes about 'Do ... s' and 'Don't ... s' under the headings.

| APPEARANCE | FIRST IMPRESSIONS | BODY LANGUAGE | QUESTIONS |

3 Which tips do you agree / disagree with? Which are the most useful?

B —

Key word
look

1 Which common multi-word verbs mean ...?
  1 to take care of someone
  2 to check something, e.g. in a dictionary
  3 to investigate

2 Complete the sentences with one of these three-part verbs.

| look up to | look down on | look forward to | look out for |

1 I'm really _____ the holidays; I just can't wait.
2 Patrick's such a snob; he _____ everyone.
3 Can you _____ a newspaper for me in town?
4 I've always _____ Charlotte; she's so good at her job.

C —

Patterns with *look*
look is followed by _____
look like is followed by _____
look like/as if is followed by _____

3 Which sentences are wrong? Correct them.

1 His boss looks like a kind man.
2 It looks as if it's going to rain.
3 The two pictures looked as if the same.
4 I don't think they look very clean.
5 He looks an airline pilot.
6 He looks like tired.

Reading
Dressing for the job

1 Put the adjectives in the right group.

POSITIVE	NEGATIVE	NEUTRAL

over-dressed	dynamic	smart	conservative	bold
assertive	elegant	neat	adventurous	unassertive
fashionable	keen	girlie	efficient	minimalist

2 Look at photos A, B, and C. Which 'look' would the following people like the most and the least? Write A, B, or C in the chart.

	Like the most	Like the least
a newspaper editor		
a headteacher of a school		
a designer		
a banker		

3 Read the article and check. What do you think of their comments?

4 What do you think the three male equivalent outfits would be?

what to wear to get that job

You get the job (or don't) within six seconds of walking into the interview. Lucy O'Brien asks four bosses, two men and two women, how they'd react to these outfits. Sarah Jackson models.

A

THE EDITOR Fine. I would probably give her a job. She looks efficient and keen. I would be quite impressed with her.

THE HEADTEACHER High heels don't make much sense in a school and a short skirt with tights is asking for trouble, quite frankly.

THE DESIGNER Fine. A lot of designers look like that, quite minimalist. Black and grey are very popular.

THE BANKER She's smart, she's fashionable, I'd employ her.

B

THE EDITOR I'd question whether she'd be adventurous enough, or bold enough as a reporter. She looks too conservative.

THE HEADTEACHER Overdressed for an interview, let alone the classroom. She looks as if she's going to a board meeting. It's executive clothing, something industrial companies would no doubt love. Extremely bright and colourful, but too smart for here.

THE DESIGNER She looks like a seventies air hostess. I'm not sure what her design work would look like – probably not very exciting.

THE BANKER What a smart, elegant young woman! She's clearly going places. You can't fault her outfit at all: neat hair, co-ordinated jewellery. And red! A good assertive colour. She'd do very well.

C

THE EDITOR Someone with no dress sense at all. I wouldn't worry too much because journalists have no dress sense.

THE HEADTEACHER Perfect. She's taken a lot of trouble with her hair, she looks comfortable, the shoes are flat, and the skirt is not provokingly short. I'd give her the job.

THE DESIGNER She looks very comfortable, which is a plus. I wouldn't say no, but she would have to wear something smarter for a client meeting.

THE BANKER She looks very unassertive. I'd worry that she isn't projecting herself as a dynamic young executive of the future if she's dressing in this girlie way.

The Independent on Sunday

a ☐ Well, when I was a student I was in charge of a group of young people at a summer camp and, as you know, adolescents can be very difficult to lead.

b ☐ I speak French and German, I think that could be extremely useful and I love anything to do with history.

c ☐ That's a difficult question. Sometimes I can get impatient with colleagues who work too slowly.

d ☐ Nobody likes to do it but if it's part of the job I suppose you just have to make the most of it.

e ☐ I was replacing someone who was on maternity leave so my contract ended when she came back.

English in use
Answering confidently

1 Match interview questions 1 to 8 with answers **a** to **h**.

Tough interview questions

1 Tell me something you're proud of.
2 What makes you think you could do this job?
3 What kind of leadership qualities do you have?
4 Why did you leave your last job?
5 Do you have any skills or hobbies you think might be useful for this job?
6 What do you think is your greatest fault?
7 How do you feel about spending time away from home?
8 What do you see yourself doing in five years' time?

f ☐ I think I've got the right background and personal qualities to do the job.

g [1] Winning the 'Employee of the month' competition three times in one year.

h ☐ I'm not really sure ... maybe I'd like to have my own business.

2 Listen and check. Which are good answers? Which are less impressive?

Sounding confident

The way we sound can be as important as what we say. In an interview you will sound more confident if you:

- project well and speak up.
- use emphatic stress on key words to make your point.
  I think that could be extremely useful.
  Winning the 'Employee of the month' competition.
- use a wide voice range (making your voice move up and down).

3 Listen again. Decide if the answer is confident (✔) or unsure (✗).

4 In pairs, ask and answer the interview questions. Be confident.

Speak out
Job interviews

Think before you speak

Interviewees

- Sound bright and confident; speak up, use stress and range.
- Avoid negative body language; look the interviewers in the eye.

Interviewers

- Show that you're interested.
- Ask for as much information as you can.
- When you are deciding at the end, use expressions with *look*.

1 Read the advertisement. What qualities do you think successful applicants for this job will need?

2 Work in two groups, interviewers and interviewees.

Interviewers Turn to *p.109*. Decide which 'tricky situations' you would like to test each of the candidates with, or invent your own.

Interviewees Spend five minutes together deciding what you will say. Think of good answers to the 'tough questions' 1 to 8. Think of a couple of questions to ask about the job at the end.

culture tours is looking for bright, lively people of all ages to accompany groups of foreign visitors on tours of your city and country.

If you think you can be a mixture of guide, diplomat, nurse-maid, and leader then we look forward to hearing from you. No formal qualifications necessary, though previous experience would be an advantage. We are most interested in the personal qualities you can bring to the job. Being a group leader with **culture tours** is a rewarding experience which you will never forget. Opportunities for full career development for the right candidates.

3 When you are ready, hold five-minute interviews.

4 Agree together who you would choose for the job, and why.

16
CATS AND RATS

In this lesson

- Extend your vocabulary to do with work.
- Look at work in different cultures.
- Practise talking about work.

Speak for yourself

1 Decide how far you agree with the following statements about work.

		Agree				Disagree
1	It's not *what* you know but *who* you know that counts.	1	2	3	4	5
2	Too many people live to work rather than work to live.	1	2	3	4	5
3	It doesn't matter what job you do, but how you do it.	1	2	3	4	5
4	I'd rather be a happy dustman than an unhappy millionaire.	1	2	3	4	5
5	Job satisfaction is more important than a good salary.	1	2	3	4	5

2 In groups, exchange views. Give examples to support your own opinions.

Reading
Words in context

1 Read the text. Which of the employment cultures described is closer to your own?

2 Do you know people who do very little but who earn a lot? Or the opposite? Think of examples of both.

3 Look at these job titles from different working environments. Which are higher and which are lower status?

administrator	clerk	personal assistant	consultant
secretary	executive	manager	president
director	partner		

FAT CATS

In Britain and the USA, the managing directors or presidents of big companies are often accused of being 'fat cats', i.e. bosses whose salaries are often twenty-five times more than the company's lowest-paid worker. When times are hard and workers are laid off, they receive very little. Departing directors, on the other hand, get big *golden handshakes*.

By contrast, in Japan the ratio between the highest and lowest paid is normally a more modest seven or eight to one. In addition, large Japanese companies have the reputation of taking care of all their employees, and the concept of a 'job for life' is still by and large true.

golden handshake
generous redundancy payment

Vocabulary
The world of work

1 Match the descriptions and definitions.

1	If a job is **stressful** …	a	you're unlikely to lose it.
2	If a job is **rewarding** …	b	it goes nowhere.
3	If a job is **challenging** …	c	it makes you feel worried.
4	If a job is **secure** …	d	it's enjoyably demanding.
5	If a job is **dead-end** …	e	it promises a good future.
6	If a job has **prospects** …	f	it gives you personal satisfaction.

2 Describe three jobs using the words in **bold**. Explain your choices.

3 Against the clock! Work in two groups, **A** and **B**.

1 Define the words in your box in three minutes.

A	
application form	part-time
references	skills
qualifications	

B	
shift work	full-time
go on strike	overtime
wages	

2 Check your answers. Group **A** turn to *p.109* and Group **B** turn to *p.111*.

3 Test a partner from the other group.

4 Rewrite the sentences using an expression from the box.

1 She **was dismissed** because she kept on arriving late.
2 He **lost his job** because the factory closed down.
3 Her brother **gets unemployment benefit**.
4 They **didn't have a job** all through the summer.
5 Her uncle **used personal contacts** to get her the job.
6 I'm looking for a **safe and ordinary** job without any surprises.
7 I've decided to **leave my job** and travel for a year.
8 Let's face facts, I'm simply not **suited to** a career in medicine.
9 She's only 23 but she **has** 30 people **working for her**.
10 We generally **employ more people** in the weeks before Christmas.

to be on the dole
to take on extra staff
to be made redundant
to be cut out for something
to get the sack
to be in charge of
to be out of work
nine-to-five
to hand in one's notice
to pull strings

5 Talk to three different people. Use as many work words/phrases as you can.

* How easy/difficult is it to find work in your country?
* What kind of work is available?
* What kinds of jobs are/would you be interested in doing?

Speak out
Joining the rat race

1 In pairs, decide where the following numbers go.

10	25	44	40,000	1,000,000

> When Bombay council announced seventy new jobs as night rat-catchers more than
> 1 _____ people applied; half of the applicants were university graduates. The salary of
> 2 £ _____ a month is paid only if 3 _____ rats are killed each night. More than
> 4 _____ students graduate each year from India's universities – the highest number in
> the world. A college education is seen as a way of changing class and caste status. After just
> 5 _____ years, a night rat-catcher can get a permanent day-time job. And as a civil
> servant it is a secure job for life! However, as Mr Shastri of Bombay council says, 'You don't
> need a *PhD* to kill a rat.'
>
> _____
> PhD one of the highest academic qualifications   *The Independent on Sunday*

Think before you speak

* Try to use at least ten vocabulary items from this lesson.
* Include examples, from your own experience or from things you've read, to strengthen your argument.

2 In pairs, decide which three groups are most affected by unemployment, and why.

SCHOOL-LEAVERS WITH FEW QUALIFICATIONS		
ARTS GRADUATES	SCIENCE GRADUATES	MIDDLE-AGED PEOPLE
IMMIGRANTS	THE DISABLED	WOMEN

17
GOING PLACES

In this lesson

- Practise making plans using the language of suggestions and preferences.
- Look at how to assert yourself and express your wishes.
- Use the technique of scanning to read a brochure effectively.

Speak for yourself

1 Write down five things you always take on holiday. Compare with a partner.

2 Quickly read how two experienced travellers pack.
   1 Which one is most like you?
   2 What would you tell the magazine about how you pack?

3 In pairs, agree on your top five items for …
   - a back-packing holiday in Thailand.
   - a week at a luxury health farm.

COLIN THUBRON
travel writer and novelist

I'm a minimalist when it comes to packing. I ask myself whether I really need something, and usually the answer is no, so I travel with literally just a change of shirt and underwear. I always take notebooks and Biros, but no camera. It turns you into a tourist. I suppose if anyone were to look in my rucksack the only things that they might be surprised at would be a few little toys that I give to the children of families I stay with; and a very small hedgehog at the bottom of the pack, which a girlfriend gave me.

LUCINDA LAMBTON
photographer, broadcaster and writer

I take every item of clothing that I possess in two big, heavy suitcases. I can't bear to leave anything behind. Suitcases should always be American because they are so strong. I have five beautiful bags with rabbits running all over them. One of them has hair grips, one has cotton wool, another has Elastoplast and painkillers, and a sewing kit. Then there's one with a toothbrush and soap, and another containing make-up. It's so comforting knowing everything I need is there.

Country Living

Reading
Scanning for information

1 What do you already know about Poland?

2 Look at the two tours of Poland on *p.49*. Mark the route of each on the map. Underline the places and sights which sound the most interesting.

3 In pairs **A** and **B**, quickly scan the text. Find out what's special about these things. Tell your partner.

Effective reading

Scanning is a useful reading skill when you are looking for key information such as names, dates, or numbers.

- Using a pencil to guide your eye, move it down the centre of the text. Circle the key information you are looking for.

A	B
Oswiecim	amber
the Tatras	the Palace of Culture
Jasna Gora	Lenin shipyards
sliwki	the Kazimierz district
Zelazowa Wola	the Kinga chapel

Baltic & Tatra mountains tour

Day 1 Gdansk Mid-morning arrival at Gdansk airport. Transfer to hotel. After lunch, sightseeing tour of Gdansk, former Prussian and Hanseatic port known as Danzig until end of WWII (looks similar to Amsterdam). Famous for the former Lenin Shipyards and the birthplace of the trade union Solidarity. Organ concert in Olive Cathedral. Dinner and overnight.

Day 2 Torun After breakfast, departure for Torun, birthplace of the astronomer Nicholaus Copernicus, via Malbork. Sightseeing tour of Malbork, including castle of Teutonic knights. Dinner and overnight.

Day 3 Warsaw After breakfast, departure for Warsaw via Zelazowa Wola, the birthplace of Frederic Chopin. Short visit to his family house. Lunch. Evening tour of Warsaw.

Day 4 Cracow Departure for Cracow via Czestochowa. Sightseeing tour of Czestochowa. Visit to Jasna Gora Monastery. Dinner and overnight in Cracow.

Day 5 Cracow After breakfast, city sightseeing tour of Cracow. Afternoon excursion to Wieliczka Salt Mine, one of the oldest salt mines in Europe. Includes the beautiful Kinga chapel carved entirely from salt. Dinner and overnight.

Day 6 Zakopane After breakfast, departure for Zakopane, a major mountain resort for skiing in winter and walking in summer. Winter festival and folklore centre in Tatras. Sightseeing tour of Zakopane. Dinner and folk display overnight.

Day 7 Cracow Very early breakfast. Departure for Cracow. Transfer to Cracow airport for evening flight to London.

Warsaw A guided tour is a must: the ghetto memorial commemorates the fate of 380,000 Jews sentenced to the horrors of Auschwitz; the colourful old town is a monument to the Polish spirit which rebuilt Warsaw's heart, including Market Square, Castle Square, and St John's Cathedral. The huge Palace of Culture was a 'gift' from Stalin. Both Marie Curie and Chopin were born here. Enjoy a summer concert in Lazienki park. The smartest shops are on Nowy Swiat; look out for caviar and sliwki (plums in chocolate).

Cracow The Wawel hill complex is a magnificent combination of gothic, baroque, and renaissance architecture. Visit the Old Town on foot: St. Mary's church, and the Bishop's Palace, home of Pope John Paul II when he was Karol Wojtyla. Cracow's Jewish heritage may still be found in the Kazimierz district, where Schindler's List was filmed. Polish specialities include bigos (sauerkraut, onion, and sausage) and fish; and don't forget the many different vodkas to try! Best buys in the Cloth Hall market are amber jewellery, leather, and carved wooden goods.

Southern tour

Day 1 Warsaw Arrival at Warsaw International airport. Transfer to hotel. Dinner and overnight.
Day 2 Cracow Breakfast. Coach drive to Cracow, former capital of Poland. A town with many architectural monuments, and a centre of culture and the arts, it is on the UNESCO list of cultural heritage. Evening city sightseeing tour of Cracow. Musical entertainment and dinner. Overnight.
Day 3 Cracow Breakfast. Walking tour of Cracow including St Mary's church with its world famous wooden altar and Wawel royal castle. After lunch, a choice of excursions to Oswiecim (Auschwitz) Concentration Camp and museum, or Wieliczka Salt Mine; one of the oldest salt mines in Europe.
Day 4 Cracow Opportunities for shopping or just relaxing. Or, if you prefer, a full one-day trip to Zakopane, Poland's famous mountain resort.
Day 5 Cracow Breakfast. Morning visits to amber jewellery and glassware workshops. After lunch, coach drive to Czestochowa. Dinner and overnight.
Day 6 Czestochowa Breakfast. Tour of Czestochowa, a place of pilgrimage, famous for its monastery at Jasna Gora. World famous portrait of Our Lady, the 'Black Madonna'. Lunch. Drive to Warsaw and overnight.
Day 7 Warsaw Breakfast. Half-day tour of Warsaw, the city almost completely devastated during WW II. Transfer to airport for evening flight to London.

4 Decide which tour you would choose, and why.

5 Explain the difference between ...

   1 'excursion' and 'journey'.   4 'resort' and 'birthplace'.
   2 'pilgrimage' and 'trip'.   5 'heritage' and 'history'.
   3 'folklore' and 'religion'.

Listening
Making choices

1 Listen to John and Barbara discussing the two tours.

   1 Which tour does each prefer?
   2 What do they finally decide to do?

2 What do these expressions mean? Check with the Tapescript on *p.116* to see how they are used.

(not) fancy	(not) keen on	(not) feel up to
could do with	do (your) own thing	

English in use
Suggestions and preferences

1 Choose the correct form of the verb. Listen and check.
 1 Let's **look**/~~to look~~ at the brochure.
 2 I'd rather **know**/**to know** one or two places well.
 3 What about **go**/**going** up to the mountains?
 4 If you really want **go**/**to go** there ...
 5 Otherwise I could **visiting**/**visit** this salt mine instead.
 6 I'd prefer **to do**/**do** that.
 7 We could always **do**/**to do** our own thing.
 8 Why don't we **hire**/**hiring** a car?
 9 How about **to give**/**giving** them a ring?
 10 We'd better **do**/**to do** it straightaway.

2 Put the expressions on the left with the correct headings from the box below. Listen again and copy the intonation.

Let's ...	I'd rather ...
What about ...	I'd prefer ...
We could always ...	How about ...
Why don't we ...	We'd better ...
Otherwise I could ... (instead)	

Suggestions and preferences

Stating preferences
Making suggestions/giving alternatives
Making suggestions with a sense of obligation

Asserting yourself

'Asserting yourself' means making your point strongly. A technique for trying to get your own way is to acknowledge and seem to agree with what someone says, but then to say something entirely different!

Yes, but ...	I know what you mean, but ...
I suppose so, but ...	I understand what you're saying ..., but ...
I'd love to ..., but ...	You're right, but ...

3 Look at the Tapescript again (*p.116*). Find out how the expressions in the box above continue.

Speak out
Doing your own thing?

1 Look at the kinds of places you can visit on a tour. Rank them in order of importance for you.

Somewhere ...

- of outstanding natural beauty.
- famous for its food and drink.
- you can buy interesting souvenirs.
- which is a site of engineering or architectural interest.
- you can experience folklore and national heritage.
- which has a connection with a great musician, poet, or writer.
- of great historic interest.
- which has good nightlife.
- you can really relax.

Think before you speak
- Use the language of suggestions and preferences accurately.
- Try to make alternative suggestions when you don't agree.
- Use the technique for asserting yourself, and try to get the others to go where you prefer.

2 In groups, turn to *p.111*. Agree on one of the holidays together.

ALL THE BEST

In this lesson

- Revise and extend uses of comparative and superlative forms.
- Practise comparing hotels, different nationalities, and holidays.
- Tell a story about an experience you've had.

Speak for yourself

1 Look at this list of hotel facilities. Add five more.

swimming pool	gymnasium	satellite TV	mini-bar
24-hour room service	conference room	disco	lifts
en-suite bathroom	laundry service	safe	fax / e-mail

2 What other things are important when choosing a hotel? Decide on the three most/least important factors for you. Compare with a partner.

3 Describe suitable hotel profiles for ...
- a business traveller.
- a couple on honeymoon.
- a family with young children.

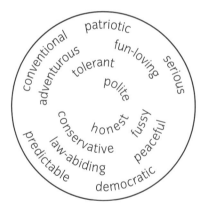

patriotic
conventional
adventurous
fun-loving
tolerant
serious
polite
honest
fussy
conservative
law-abiding
peaceful
predictable
democratic

Reading
Evaluating a text

1 Find words from the circle to describe ...
  1 someone who likes to enjoy life.
  2 someone who expects every detail to be perfect.
  3 someone who has a great respect for rules and regulations.

2 In pairs, define the other adjectives.

3 Look at the photo below. What is a 'tourist trap'?

4 Read **Part 1** of the text. What is the 'trap' described here?

Part 1

'This place has always been a real tourist trap.'

Tourist trap

Everybody knows that different nationalities have their own special behaviour when they go on holiday. The Germans use their towels to reserve the sun-beds by the swimming pool, the Americans are the loudest, the Japanese are quiet and polite, while the British are almost permanently drunk. But these stereotypes are challenged by a TV documentary series. Psychologists created some tests to show the best and worst sides of tourists from all four countries. Then, groups of holidaymakers were secretly filmed at a hotel in Turkey, and their behaviour examined.

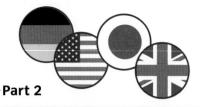

5 In pairs, read **Part 2** of the text. **A** find out about the British and the Americans, **B** find out about the Germans and the Japanese. Make notes about the nationalities.

| GERMANS | AMERICANS | JAPANESE | BRITISH |

Part 2

The Germans were the only group to send back a bottle of wine tasting of vinegar, the British did not mind when people jumped the queue, and the Japanese were so shocked when an actor began showering in the nude that they turned their backs on him. The most upsetting thing for the Americans was finding someone had burned their flag.

There were also surprising reactions to a 'drunk' coach driver. The British were the least accepting and refused to get on the bus. The Japanese weren't worried until their group leader noticed that the driver had a bottle of alcohol. The Germans were by far the most understanding and did not want to make a fuss in case the driver lost his job.

When the tourists had a free afternoon the British played football in the pouring rain, the Germans went walking, the Japanese hired a coach to go sight-seeing, and the Americans played pool.

In one situation an actor started smoking on a no-smoking bus. The British politely asked him to smoke outside, the Japanese were far more concerned with maintaining harmony and said nothing, the Germans had a vote and asked him to put it out, while the Americans were the least bothered, and actually started smoking themselves.

All four nationalities were as accepting as each other when they were served deliberately poor food. When an actor pretended to steal beer from the bar the British and Americans were no better than each other and started to join in. The Germans refused to take part, while the Japanese were so horrified that they told the bar staff.

The programme makers agreed that the Germans were the most serious group. During a toga evening they reluctantly took part only when they were given clean sheets. Hotel staff judged the Japanese as the most fun-loving.

The Guardian

6 What do you think of the tests? How would you have reacted?

Comparatives and superlatives

Grammar revisited

1 Find examples of different types of comparative and superlative forms in the text. Match them to similar examples in the Summary on *p.53*.

2 Complete the sentences using a modifier and a comparative/superlative form.

1 The Japanese are _____ polite than the other nationalities.

2 The British drink _____ the Americans.

3 The Americans are _____ patriotic.

4 The Germans are _____ honest than the British and Americans.

3 Make comparisons of your own between the four different nationalities using the adjectives from the circle on *p.51*.

Grammar plus

> • Use comparatives to give a sense of progression.
>   *It got worse and worse as the night went on.*
> • Use superlatives and the present perfect to talk about your most memorable experiences.
>   *It's the worst place I've ever stayed in.*

4 Make true sentences about these topics.

1 City centres …
   are becoming more and more polluted.

2 Crime …

3 Houses / flats …

4 The weather …

5 Public transport …

5 Make questions from these prompts.

1 good meal / ever eat
   What's the best meal you've ever eaten?

2 bad hotel / ever stay in

3 frightening experience / ever have

4 big mistake / ever make

5 bad journey / ever go on

⏱ Against the clock!

Set a time limit

6 In pairs, decide on three more questions for ex.5. Ask and answer the questions and make notes about as many experiences as you can.

Listening
Following a narrative

1 Listen to Tamsin telling Marina about her experiences in a hotel. What problems did she have with ...?

   1 the bed   **2** the bathroom   **3** noise

2 What action did she take?

Speak out
Hotel

1 In small groups, invent a story based around one of these hotels, or tell a story that really happened to one of you. Include ...

- something funny/frightening/embarrassing/strange that happened.
- an incident that happened while you were travelling to or leaving the hotel.
- some nice/awful people you met.

Think before you speak

- Practise different comparative and superlative forms.
- Include a comparative to give a sense of progression, e.g. *louder and louder*.
- Include a superlative with *ever*, e.g. *the worst place I've ever stayed in*.

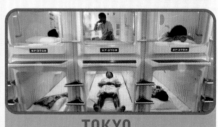

ARCTIC
cold water only, although there is a nearby sauna, and the beds are made of ice

BENIDORM
very hot, disco till late, lots of young people

TOKYO
centre of Tokyo, own TV/video/radio, shared bathroom facilities

2 In new groups, tell each other your stories.

SUMMARY

Comparative adjectives

- *Stereos are cheaper than they used to be.*
- *Rome is usually much hotter than London.*
- *This book is more interesting than the last one I read.*
- *I'm feeling worse than I did yesterday.*

Superlative adjectives

- *Yesterday was the hottest day of the year so far.*
- *That's probably the most/least expensive restaurant in town.*
- *That is the best ice-cream I've ever tasted.*

as ... as

- *Tom is almost as tall as his brother now.*
- *Our holiday wasn't quite as expensive as I thought it would be.*

Quantifiers

- With plural countable nouns use *fewer*.
  The Galaxy has fewer rooms than the Astoria.
- With uncountable nouns use *less*.
  I'm trying to drink less coffee than I used to.

Modifiers

- *Miranda's sight is slightly/a little bit worse than Andrea's.*
- *He plays tennis far/much/a lot better than his younger brother.*
- *Her cooking is even worse than mine!*
- *Mike is by far the best dancer here.*

Comparative adverbs

- *He drives more slowly than his wife.*
- *He has to work a lot harder now than he used to.*
- *All my colleagues can type much faster than me.*

19
SO MANY QUESTIONS

In this lesson

- Practise ways of asking and answering questions politely.
- Focus on how to avoid answering personal questions.
- Look at the appropriacy of personal questions.

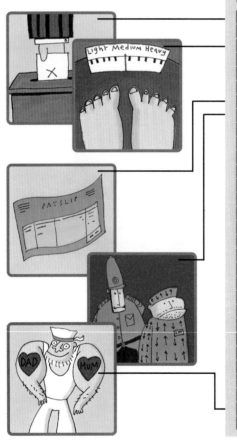

Speak for yourself

1 How comfortable are you answering personal questions?

2 Look at the list of personal questions. Tick the ones you would be prepared to answer in public. Compare with a partner.

Speaking personally

1. Which party did you vote for at the last election?
2. How much do you weigh?
3. What is your favourite film or book?
4. Who would look after your child if it was sick?
5. Do you believe in angels?
6. How much do you earn?
7. Have you ever been in trouble with the police?
8. What would you change about your appearance?
9. Under what circumstances would you hit a child?
10. What is your greatest fault?
11. Are you in a strong and lasting relationship?
12. Are you planning to start a family?
13. How many days have you taken off work in the last three years?
14. Will you give us permission to look at your medical records?
15. Have you ever been a member of a trade union?
16. Which person from history do you most admire?
17. How many hours do you like to sleep at night?
18. Are you colour blind?
19. Do you believe in life after death?
20. What is your greatest fear?
21. Would you ever give your home number to an important client?
22. Have you ever had mental health problems?
23. Would you be prepared to lie or die for your country?
24. Do/did you love your parents?
25. What's your favourite colour?

3 Decide which questions would be justified in the following situations.
- a social worker to a couple wishing to adopt a child
- a soldier or a diplomat who is being selected for a difficult mission
- an insurance company to a client who is asking for life insurance cover
- an employer to a prospective employee
- someone who wanted to share a flat with you

4 Are there any questions that should never be asked?

Listening
Avoiding the question

 1 Look back at the first eight questions on *p.54*. Listen, and tick if they answer the question, cross if they don't.

2 Listen again. What kind of reply do they give to each question? Is it 'polite', 'aggressive', or 'humorous'?

Don't ask me how old I am!

English in use
Less direct questions

We can soften what we ask by making our questions less direct.

How old are you? = Would you mind telling me how old you are?

I wonder if you could tell me _____

I'd like you to tell me _____

I'd like to know _____

Would you mind telling me _____

Do you think you could tell me _____

---

 1 Listen and complete the phrases in the box.

2 What differences in structure and word order do you notice between the direct and less direct questions?

Avoiding the question

If a question is too personal you can simply refuse to answer it.

    If you don't mind, I'd rather not say.

Otherwise a good technique is to avoid answering, or say you don't know.

    I've never really thought about it.
    I haven't the faintest idea.

Refusing to answer

    Now that _____ .
    I'd prefer _____ .
    Mind _____ .

Saying you don't know

    I haven't _____ .
    I've got _____ .

Avoiding answering

    That's a _____ .
    I'll have _____ .
    That's a rather _____ .

---

 3 Complete the expressions in the box. Listen and check.

4 Listen again and copy the intonation.

5 In pairs, turn to the Tapescript on *p.116*. Practise the exchanges in Listening 1.

The Questionnaire

1 **With which historical figure do you most identify?**
The blind musician Ah Bing, because of his music.

2 **What vehicle do you own?**
A bicycle.

3 **What is your greatest extravagance?**

4 **What objects do you always carry with you?**
An army satchel.

5 **What makes you most depressed?**
Dealing with record companies.

6 **What do you most dislike about your appearance?**

7 **What is your most unappealing habit?**
I am incapable of being punctual.

8 **What is your favourite smell?**

9 **What is your favourite building?**
The Bell and Drum Tower in Beijing.

10 **What is your favourite journey?**
Travelling by train in south-west China.

11 **What or who is the greatest love of your life?**
Musical instruments, especially electronic ones.

12 **Which living person do you most despise?**
It has to be myself because I am so impossible.

13 **What is your greatest regret?**

14 **When and where were you happiest?**
In my dreams.

15 **What single thing would improve the quality of your life?**

16 **Which talent would you most like to have?**
Extra-sensory powers.

17 **What would your motto be?**
'Serve the people' (a quotation from Mao Ze-dong).

18 **How would you like to be remembered?**
For my music.

Reading
Making connections

1 The Chinese rock singer He Yong was interviewed by *The Guardian* newspaper. Look at five of his answers. What were the questions?

1 The smell of things after it has just rained.
2 That I was not born a girl. I'm certain I would have been very pretty.
3 My own apartment.
4 Smoking and drinking.
5 My legs.

2 Match the answers to the questionnaire.

The Guardian

Glossary

1 An _____ is something expensive that you can't really afford.
2 Someone who is _____ is never late.
3 If you _____ someone or something you disapprove of it strongly.
4 A _____ is a special natural ability or gift.
5 A _____ is a 'saying' that you try to live your life by.

3 Complete the Glossary with words from the text.
4 Which of his answers did you find the most interesting or surprising?
5 Were there any questions you wouldn't have wanted to answer?

Speak out
Personal questions

Think before you speak
* Be sensitive about the kinds of questions you ask.
* Use a variety of question forms, both direct and indirect.
* Use the techniques for refusing to answer and avoiding the question if you don't want to reply.

1 Choose any ten questions from this lesson.
2 In pairs, take turns to ask and answer the questions you have chosen.
3 What's the most interesting answer you got?

20 WHO DO YOU THINK YOU ARE?

In this lesson

- Extend your knowledge of adjectives to do with personality.
- Practise expressing opinions about your country.
- Look at where you would choose to live, and why.

Speak for yourself

1 Read the survey. Choose from the three countries.

What do Europeans really think of each other?

Here are the results of a recent survey. Which country was thought to ...?

1	have the best quality of life	Austria ☐	France ☐	Sweden ☐
2	be the best place for a holiday	Spain ☐	Greece ☐	France ☐
3	have the most attractive people	Italy ☐	Sweden ☐	Greece ☐
4	have the most trustworthy people	Germany ☐	Denmark ☐	Italy ☐
5	have the nicest, most fun people	Germany ☐	Italy ☐	Greece ☐
6	have the highest standard of living	Britain ☐	Germany ☐	Belgium ☐
7	produce the best quality goods	France ☐	Germany ☐	Britain ☐
8	have the worst food	Britain ☐	Portugal ☐	Holland ☐

2 Turn to *p.109* and check. Were you right? Did anything surprise you?

3 How would you answer the questions (including all countries)?

Vocabulary
Character and attitudes

HOLLAND

PORTUGAL

LIVERPOOL

1 **Against the clock!** In groups, decide if the adjectives are 'Positive', 'Negative', or 'Neutral', in five minutes. Use a dictionary if you wish.

old-fashioned	attractive	reserved	distant
lively	racist	tolerant	sophisticated
arrogant	down-to-earth	suspicious	welcoming
modest	polite	cosmopolitan	forward-thinking
intense	open	conformist	narrow-minded
romantic	superficial	easy-going	trustworthy
genuine	melancholy	narcissistic	behind-the-times
provincial	egalitarian	individualist	sensitive

2 How easy was it to agree?

3 Find words which follow these stress patterns.

Oo (e.g. **live**ly)	oOo	Ooo	oO

4 Draw stress patterns for these words.

superficial	sophisticated	cosmopolitan
narrow-minded	melancholy	

5 Make a character profile for your nationality. In pairs turn to *p.109*.

Paul Segersvaro 39, optician
Helsinki (Finland)

Our seasons are good for the soul. When spring comes after the dark days of winter you feel you are being reborn. Because summer is so short there is a sense of desperate living before winter closes in. The darkness gives you time to spend leisure time with your friends. I also love the birdlife.
Favourite alternative Costa Rica because it's good for birds.

Ria Vandenhaute 47, bank teller
Berg (Belgium)

Openness to new things and people is the best thing. And I like our family values: we are very attached to our houses and gardens. There is a saying that each Belgian has a brick in him.
Favourite alternative Australia because you can change jobs, location, lifestyle really easily, while here our lives are quite rigid.

Reading
Opinions

1 Say three things you like/don't like about your country.

2 Read the texts. Think of one adjective to describe each person.

Tina Joyce 19, student
Liverpool (England)

People are much more welcoming and friendly in the north. In Liverpool, which used to be a great port, the population is so mixed that people aren't racist. I would say that we're not sophisticated, but we are very tolerant and down-to-earth, which is much more important.
Favourite alternative New York for its job opportunities and nightlife.

Camilla Brattnäs 24, policewoman
Stockholm (Sweden)

As a young woman, I can get a job and earn my own living. I also appreciate our social security system. It's difficult to become homeless in Sweden.
Favourite alternative Britain, especially London. It's a beautiful city and I like the language.

Michiko Sato 24, teacher
Osaka (Japan)

It's safe here. A woman can travel alone, even at night, without being afraid. Your family and colleagues care about you. This is very comforting.
Favourite alternative Denmark because it's less conformist and predictable than Japan. Sometimes it can be very intense here. There is a lot of group pressure to make you accept things you do not like.

Ana Pinto-Coelho 23, accountant
Lisbon (Portugal)

I like the fact that the sea makes us melancholy. The Atlantic makes you dream of far-off places. It makes you look outwards. The Mediterranean makes you narcissistic.
Favourite alternative Rome or Milan because they have open minds.

The European

3 Whose attitudes are closest to your own? Which person would you most/least like to sit next to on a long journey?

4 How important are geography and climate in forming national character?

Speak out
Make the break

1 In pairs, imagine you and your partner have to move abroad and stay in a country of your choice for one year.

  1 Decide on the three most and least important considerations.

  2 Are there any others you would like to add?

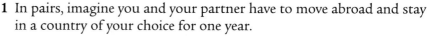

I would choose somewhere which ...

1 reminds me of home.	8 has a language I feel comfortable with.
2 is unpolluted and unspoilt.	9 has good education and welfare for everyone.
3 has a good standard of living.	
4 is safe and crime-free.	10 has a lively music scene and interesting culture.
5 has beautiful, fashionable people.	
6 has good food and drink.	11 has strong family values.
7 lets me be 'me' (i.e. lets me live my life openly).	12 guarantees me political and religious freedom.

2 Agree where to go. Explain your choices to another pair.

3 Decide how your choices might change if you were moving for the rest of your life.

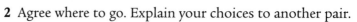

21 FESTIVAL

In this lesson

- Look at the structure of a talk.
- Practise recognizing and using language signals in a talk.
- Use expressions with the key word *take*.

Speak for yourself

1 Are there any interesting festivals in your town or country?
2 Read the short descriptions of two very different festivals.
  1 Which one do you think is more unusual?
  2 Which one would you most / least like to watch?
  3 Which one would you most / least like to participate in?

THE BULL RUN

Where Pamplona, Spain
When 7th July

What happens During the festival of San Fermín, locals and tourists run through the town chased by a herd of bulls in the annual *encierro* or bull run. At 8.00 a.m. a rocket signals the release of the bulls, which charge the 800m across town to the bull ring where the afternoon's bullfight takes place. The tradition started when farmers bringing bulls to the fights would camp outside the city the night before, then drive their animals through the streets to the ring the next morning.

Focus magazine

MIDSOMMAR

Where throughout Sweden
When the nearest Friday to 24th June

What happens On Midsummer's eve a maypole is decorated. It's a pagan celebration of light, warmth, and nature. The day begins with traditional dancing followed by games. People eat herring, new potatoes, and strawberries, and drink beer and schnapps. A night of supernatural powers.

The European

Listening
Following a talk

1 Look at photos **A** to **D** of *Hina Matsuri*. Describe what you can see.
2 Listen to Cathy talking to a group of colleagues about the festival of *Hina Matsuri*. Match photos **A** to **D** to the four stages of her talk.
3 Listen again. Complete the notes for each photo.
4 Quickly tell a partner about the festival using the photos and notes.

A	B	C	D
			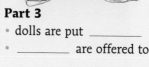

Part 1
- a _____ festival
- takes place on _____
- dedicated to _____

Part 2
- dolls dressed in _____
- dolls given to _____ by _____

Part 3
- dolls are put _____
- _____ are offered to _____

Part 4
- dolls are put _____
- bad luck is _____ with the dolls

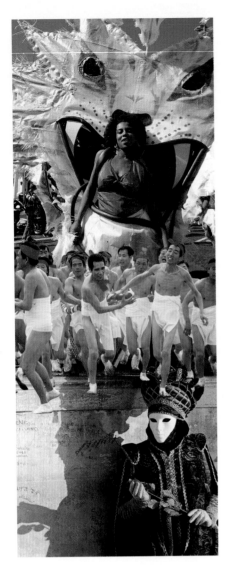

English in use

Signals

When you are listening to someone giving a talk, recognizing 'language signals' will help you to predict the kind of things the speaker is about to say.

Anyway, the dolls are put into boats and ...

You see, the idea is that bad luck is taken away ...

1 Highlight the four signals **a** to **d** in the Tapescript on *pp.116/117*. What follows?

a Right then ...

b Anyway ...

c Incidentally ...

d You see ...

2 Which of the signals ...?

1 shows that you are about to start ☐

2 is an introduction to an explanation ☐

3 shows that you are ready to continue ☐

4 is an introduction to extra information ☐

Repetition

Repetition is often used to describe a state which is changing.

Fewer and fewer people are spending their summer holidays in Britain.

Sometimes we use it for emphasis.

There were **hundreds and hundreds** of people at the party.

3 Look at the Tapescript again (*pp.116/117*). Complete the sentences.

1 _____ of girls are given a set of dolls.

2 This one has got _____ .

3 _____ people come each year.

4 Listen and copy the intonation. Which words are stressed? What happens to *and*?

5 Continue these sentences. Use the correct intonation.

1 Lots and lots of people are worried about ...

2 I don't understand why fewer and fewer women ...

3 There were thousands and thousands of ...

4 Parents are spending less and less time ...

5 More and more money ...

Key word
take

Diagram connected to **TAKE**:
- (it / something) for granted
- an interest in
- place (in / on)
- advantage of
- (something) away
- care of
- pride in
- part in

1 Complete these expressions from the Tapescript (*pp.116 / 117*).

1 It _____ each year on 3rd March.

2 Many Japanese girls _____ the festival.

3 They _____ enormous _____ them.

4 They _____ a great deal of _____ the display.

5 This kind of perfection is just _____ in Japan.

2 Complete the sentences below with an expression with *take*.

1 I used to _____ that we would go to the circus each year.

2 The person who made that beautiful costume really _____ their work.

3 She really _____ her pet rabbit although she's only six.

4 The World Cup _____ every four years.

5 Are you going to _____ this year's carnival, Ana?

6 I wish he'd _____ something other than football.

7 Raymond _____ their friendship to advance his career.

8 _____ it _____ ! I don't like it!

3 Make a true sentence with each expression.

4 Use a dictionary. Add more expressions with *take* to the diagram.

Speak out
Talking about a special event

Give a short talk about a festival or special event from your own country or region. Work on your own, or in small groups. Before you begin, make notes under these headings.

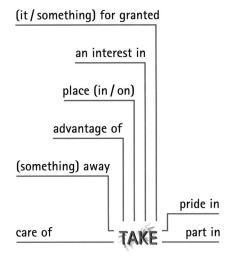

Think before you speak
- Use the organization of Cathy's talk as a guide.
- Include 'signals' to show changes in topic or different stages of the talk.
- Use repetition to describe change, or for emphasis.
- Try to include expressions with *take*.

The name of the event / festival
- where it's held
- when it takes place and how long it lasts
- what it celebrates / the reasons for the event
- who takes part

Its origins (if known)
- what special preparations it needs, i.e. costumes / decorations
- food and drink

How it begins
- what happens during the event / its atmosphere
- how it ends
- how the event has changed over the years

22
EUREKA!

In this lesson

- Revise and extend uses of the passive.
- Focus on *have/get something done*.
- Practise discussing past and future inventions.

Speak for yourself

Look at the photos of three inventions.

1 What do you think each one is for?
2 How useful do you think they are? Which ones would you use?

1

2

3

Reading
Summarizing a text

Effective reading

When you want to summarize and retell information you have read, take brief notes.

- Organize your notes into stages.
- Pick out key words and phrases.
- Use abbreviations, e.g. *possible = poss.*, *something = sthg.*

1 Look at the texts on *p.63* about how three everyday objects were invented. In groups of three, **A** read Text A, **B** read Text B, **C** read Text C. Complete the chart for your invention only.

	Text A	Text B	Text C
1 Object			
2 Inventor			
3 Inspiration			
4 Stages of development			

2 Tell the others in your group about how your object was invented.

3 Match these words and phrases from the texts with their meanings.

1	to set up a company	a	to produce in a factory
2	a version	b	a document giving right of ownership
3	to buy the rights (to sthg)	c	to be forced to stop trading
4	mass production	d	making lots of something in a factory
5	to go out of business	e	to begin a new business
6	a patent	f	another similar one
7	to manufacture	g	to pay to own and use (sthg)
8	to market (sthg)	h	to advertise and sell (sthg)

Text A

When William Russell Frisbie set up the Frisbie Pie Company at Bridgeport, Connecticut, in 1871, he can't have imagined that 100 years later his product would be responsible for a game which is now played all round the world. The Frisbie bakery was near the University of Yale. Students enjoyed eating the pies and then throwing the empty tins to one another. In 1948 these tins came to the attention of Los Angeles building inspector Fred Morrison, who created a plastic version called 'Morrison's Flying Saucer'. He had the name changed to 'Frisbee', to avoid legal difficulties. The Frisbee proved so popular among young Americans that in 1957 the Wham-O company bought the rights from Morrison. Soon beaches and parks were full of people demonstrating their Frisbee skills. Just one year after Wham-O began mass production of the Frisbee, the Frisbie Pie Company went out of business.

Text B

In 1950, while out hunting, the Swiss Georges de Mestral noticed that his trousers and the ears of his dog were covered with 'burrs', the prickly heads of plants. When he examined the heads under a microscope he saw that the outside was made up of lots of tiny hooks which stuck to anything that was passing. A broken zip fastener on his wife's dress had once ruined an evening out, and he realized that hooks could be the basis of an alternative system. After an unsuccessful start, de Mestral was introduced to Jakob Müller, a loom-manufacturer. Their product was eventually patented under the name of 'Velcro'. The name comes from the French words *velour* and *crochet* meaning 'hooked velvet'. Velcro consists of two nylon tapes, one covered in tiny loops, the other in tiny hooks. Today Velcro is manufactured around the globe, and enough Velcro tape is sold to stretch twice around the world.

Text C

The 'Post-it' note was a classic example of a product waiting for a use. In 1970, Spencer Silver was working as a research chemist with the American 3M corporation working on adhesives. He was asked to create the strongest glue on the market, but by accident developed one which could be used on any material without leaving a mark. Nobody at 3M was interested in it, until nearly ten years later a colleague of Silver's, Arthur Fry, used the adhesive to keep pieces of paper in a book. He had finally found a use for Silver's invention, and in 1981 3M marketed small blank notes with Silver's glue along one edge, calling them 'Post-it' notes. Now, no office can do without them.

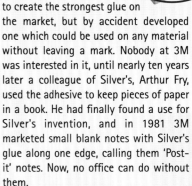

The Guinness Book of Innovations

Forms of the passive

Grammar revisited

1 Highlight examples of the passive in the texts you have just read.
  1 How is the passive formed?
  2 Choose three examples and decide why the passive is used.
  3 Why isn't the agent (i.e. the person/thing that does the action) included?

2 Rewrite the sentences in the passive. One cannot be changed. Why not?
  1 Fred Morrison created a plastic version of the Frisbee.
  2 William Russell Frisbie died before his product was famous.
  3 A broken zip ruined de Mestral's evening out.
  4 Spencer Silver invented a new type of glue.
  5 Arthur Fry developed Silver's invention.

3 Check your answers in the Summary on *p.64*.

Grammar plus

4 Why are the verbs *have* and *get* used in these sentences?
  1 I **had** my car fixed before I went on holiday.
  2 I'm going to **have** my eyes tested tomorrow.
  3 I must **get** my watch repaired.
  4 **Get** your hair cut! It looks a real mess.

5 In pairs make a list of things you usually *have/get done*.

Causative verbs
- Use *have/get something done* for actions which are done for, not by, the subject.
  I had my carpets cleaned recently.
- Use *get something done* if the situation is less formal, or with imperatives.
  Get your shoes repaired! They're falling apart.

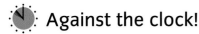

⏱ Against the clock!

Set a time limit

6 Complete the dialogues using the words in brackets and *have / get something done* or a passive form.

1 A Why did you come on the train?
   B (My car / steal / last night)

2 A Your hair looks nice.
   B (I / cut / new salon last week)

3 A How's work at the moment?
   B (Terrible / new computer system / just / install)

4 A What happened in the court case yesterday?
   B (Mr Brown / give / five year prison sentence)

5 A Their new house is in a terrible state.
   B (Yes, but they / decorate / before they move in)

6 A Did you hear about that accident?
   B (Yes, two people / injure)

7 A What happened to Martin's face?
   B (His nose / break / fight last night)

8 A You look a bit upset. What's happened?
   B (We / our dog / put to sleep yesterday evening)

9 A Did John go to the doctor?
   B (Yes, he / tell / stay at home for three days)

Speak out
Sales pitch

1 In groups, think of or invent a product and prepare to sell it to another group. Decide ...

- how it was invented
- where it's made
- how it works
- the advantages of owning it
- its price / value for money

2 'Sell' your product to another group.

Think **before you speak**

- Try to use passive forms correctly to describe products and processes.
- Include technical vocabulary if you can to describe your product in a 'professional' way.
- Be enthusiastic and persuasive about the features of your product.

SUMMARY

The passive

Form

subject + *be* (in an appropriate tense) + past participle (+ the agent)
*This book **was written** by my grandfather.*

Use

- to focus on the object of an active sentence rather than the subject.
  That lion over there ate an explorer.
  The famous explorer was eaten by a lion.
- to make something impersonal / formal.
  Passengers are requested to proceed to Gate 12.

- when the agent of an action is unknown.
  The shaduf was invented in Ancient Egypt.
- to describe processes.
  The newspapers are printed in London and then sent to distributors.

Avoid the passive

- with intransitive verbs (verbs without a direct object).
  e.g. *die, disappear, sit, sleep, get up*

Avoid using the agent

- when it is not important to the sentence
- when it is obvious
- when it has already been mentioned

23
A GOLDEN AGE?

In this lesson

- Look at how to follow and give a guided tour.
- Use expressions with the key word *get*.
- Focus on language for describing historical events, processes, and past habits and states.

Speak for yourself

1 Read this short text about Britain in the 19th century. What was good and bad about living then?

2 Underline three words or phrases with a positive connotation, and three with a negative connotation.

3 In which period of history would you have liked to live most?

Britain's 'golden age' is often considered to be the second half of the nineteenth century, when Queen Victoria was on the throne. Its Royal Navy ruled the waves, while its technical achievements and industrial revolution had made it the world's richest country. It could also be proud of its great novelists, like Charles Dickens.

However, there was a darker side. Life was desperately hard if you worked in one of the mines or factories, or lived in poverty in the slums of London or Manchester. Infant mortality was high, and diseases like typhoid, cholera, and tuberculosis used to kill thousands. Life expectancy for all classes was still only about 45 years.

Listening
Following a guided tour

eye

needle

point

1 You are going to listen to the introduction to a guided tour. Look at the pictures.
   1 What kind of place is it?
   2 How old is it?
   3 What was made there?

2 Listen to **Part A** and check your answers.

3 Listen to the complete tour.
   1 Listen to **Part A** again. Write 'true' or 'false'.
      1 The manufacturing process was invented by the Moors.
      2 The mill started in the seventeenth century.
      3 The needle mill replaced the blacksmith's forge.
      4 The machinery was powered by steam.

   2 Listen to **Part B**.
      1 Where were the needles made?
      2 Why was the factory known as 'the Fountain'?
      3 What happened in the mill?
      4 How many needles was it producing at the end of the 1800s?

1
2

3 Listen to **Part C**. Explain how the tools in pictures 1 and 2 were used.
4 Listen to **Part D**.
  1 Make notes about the job of a 'pointer'.

| DANGERS | PROTECTION | WAGES | LIFE EXPECTANCY |

  2 What shocking story does Sue tell?

4 Turn to the Tapescript on *p.117*.
  Think of a title for each of the
  four stages of her talk.
5 Which forms does she use to
  describe ...?
  1 processes
  2 past habits and states

A POINTER

English in use
Managing your audience

1 Try to complete the expressions she uses in these categories. Look at
  the Tapescript again (*p.117*) and check.

Showing you're ready

_____ morning / _____ / evening everyone.

I'd like to _____ to ... All _____ . Is everyone _____ ?

Referring to where you are

We're standing now _____ ... Pointing _____ in this mill ...

Getting people to look

_____ you can see ... I'd like _____ attention to ...

Signalling new stages

First _____ I'm going to ... I'd now like to _____ ...

_____ tell you a little bit about ...

Giving a polite order

_____ follow me ... Now if you'd like to _____ .

_____ round.

Giving warnings

Watch _____ , _____ of the low ceiling.

Involving your audience

2 During the talk Sue asks the audience several questions. What are
  they? Why do you think she asks them?
3 Why does she tell the anecdote about the man who drowned?

Key word

get

□ to become   □ to earn
□ to arrive   □ to obtain
□ own/possess
□ to ask/force someone to do something
□ when something happens to you (often unpleasant)

1 Match examples 1 to 7 to the different meanings of *get*.

1 But the technique didn't **get** to England until the 1600s.
2 ... the pub where they **got** the materials.
3 People often **got** hurt ...
4 And what's our pointer **got** to protect himself?
5 Pointers **got** six times the average wage ...
6 Pollution is **getting** worse and worse.
7 Lisa **got** me to do her ironing for her.

2 Look at the examples above again.

1 What follows *get* in sentence 3? Can you think of other examples?
2 What follows *get* in sentence 7? Write a true sentence using this construction.

3 In pairs, practise responding with *get*.

1 How are you feeling today? Not too bad ...
2 How much does she earn in that restaurant? I think ...
3 Could you ask Cindy to ring her sister? Sure, I'll ...
4 What time does this train arrive in Barcelona? It ...
5 Why is the postman afraid of your little dog? Because ...
6 Where did you find that lovely jacket? I ...
7 Is it true that he is on such a high salary? Yes, he ...

Used to

used to + base form describes discontinued past actions or states.

There **used to be** a blacksmith's forge on this site.

used to + *-ing* form describes what people are/were accustomed to doing.

People were **used to** mak**ing** needles by hand.

get used to + *-ing* form describes what people became accustomed to doing.

Pointers had to **get used to** working in dusty, noisy conditions.

Speak out
Showing people around

Think **before you speak**

- Manage your audience. Use expressions to signal what you're talking about.

- Involve your audience. Ask questions, be lively and animated, speak clearly.

- Use the correct language for describing past events and processes (passives, *used to*).

- Try to include expressions with *get*.

1 Individually, or in pairs/groups, choose a place you think would be of interest to a group of visitors to your town or place of work.

2 Make your own 'flow chart' and refer to it during your 'tour'. Group the stages of your tour according to the stages of Sue's talk.

→ welcome your guests and introduce yourself
→ tell them the plan/schedule of the visit
→ give an overview of the place of interest
→ put the place in its historical context
→ draw people's attention to interesting features or exhibits
→ refer to machinery/pictures/diagrams to illustrate your tour; describe something in detail
→ tell an interesting story associated with the place

3 Take people on your 'tour'.

24
THE WAY TO DO IT

In this lesson

- Extend your vocabulary to do with equipment.
- Look at attitudes towards new technology.
- Practise giving instructions.

Speak for yourself

1 Look at the cartoon below. What does it mean?
2 Do the questionnaire. Discuss your choices with a partner. Compare attitudes to technology.

Technophile OR technophobe?

1 How often do you use the following pieces of equipment?

a every day   b once a week   c once a month   d never

	a	b	c	d
a microwave	a☐	b☐	c☐	d☐
a fax machine	a☐	b☐	c☐	d☐
a personal computer	a☐	b☐	c☐	d☐
a modem	a☐	b☐	c☐	d☐
a CD-ROM	a☐	b☐	c☐	d☐
a camcorder	a☐	b☐	c☐	d☐
a cash machine	a☐	b☐	c☐	d☐
a mobile phone	a☐	b☐	c☐	d☐
a photocopier	a☐	b☐	c☐	d☐
an answering machine	a☐	b☐	c☐	d☐
a video player/recorder	a☐	b☐	c☐	d☐

2 What other equipment do you use regularly?

3 When you buy new equipment do you ...?
  a choose the most sophisticated model
  b choose the cheapest model
  c choose the nicest colour

4 How long does it take you to learn how to use a new piece of equipment?
  a average
  b less time than average
  c longer than average

5 How often do you feel frustrated or angry with equipment?
  a nearly every time you use it
  b only when it goes wrong
  c hardly ever

You can't teach an old dog new tricks.

Vocabulary
Technically speaking

1 What are the following means of identification?

a PIN number	a bar code	an ID card	a password

2 What do you associate the following with?
  1 on line, password, download (information), search
  2 fast forward, rewind, pause, programme
  3 save (a file), print out, key in, back up
  4 PIN number, cashcard, withdraw (money), balance enquiry
  5 in box, message, attachment, address
  6 zoom (in/out), viewfinder, window, lens

3 **Against the clock!** In pairs, match the numbers on the computer diagram to the words in the box in two minutes.

mouse	keyboard	screen	monitor	floppy disk/diskette
printer	mouse mat	cursor	disk drive	window

4 Match the original definitions to their newer meanings.

  a **a mouse** a small rodent with a tail
  b **to click** make a short hard sound
  c **an icon** a religious symbol
  d **to drag** pull something heavy
  e **to scan** read something quickly

  1 a small picture on a computer screen
  2 copy by passing an electronic beam over something
  3 press the button on a computer mouse
  4 move something on a computer screen
  5 a small device moved across a mat which controls the cursor

Listening
Words in context

1 Listen to five conversations. What's happening in each one?

2 Listen again. Note down useful ways of giving instructions.

3 Listen to these extracts from Conversation 1 again.

  1 Complete the gaps.

    a Right, _____ put it into the drive here. _____ .
    b Now, with the mouse, _____ the cursor across.
    c OK, now drag it over to the disk icon. _____ .
    d _____ , go up to the 'Special' menu and select 'Eject Disk'.
    e And _____ .

  2 Which expressions introduce an instruction?
  3 Which form of the verb does she use most of the time?

4 Complete the 'position' expressions in **bold** with one word.

  1 Your skirt is **inside** _____ ; I can see the label.
  2 Oh dear, I think they've hung that picture **upside** _____ .
  3 It won't work; you've put the batteries in the **wrong way** _____ .
  4 Your pullover's on **back to** _____ ; put it on the **right way** _____ .

Ordering instructions

Avoid using *after* on its own because you will have to follow it with the *-ing* form or change tense. It's much safer to use *then*, *afterwards*, and *after that*.

Speak out
This is what you do

1 In pairs, tell your partner how to do each task in one minute.
  • tie shoelaces
  • drink a glass of water
  • put on a pullover
  • make a sandwich

2 In pairs, work out clear instructions for one of the following. Ask another pair to listen.
  • Show how to operate a piece of office equipment, e.g. a photocopier.
  • Show how to work a piece of household equipment, e.g. a dishwasher.
  • Teach someone how to cook a local dish or perform a local dance.
  • Explain how to make something from a piece of paper.

Think before you speak
• Introduce your instructions with *Right, Now, OK*, etc. to make them sound natural.
• Use ordering and positioning expressions to make your instructions clear.
• Use the right technical vocabulary.

In this lesson

- Practise giving opinions.
- Use emphatic stress to make a point.
- Use expressions with the key word *thing*.

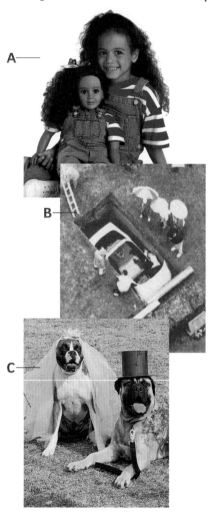

A

B

C

Effective reading

Newspaper language often carries messages which tell you about the attitude of the writer.

- Look at the headlines and see if you can find jokes or word play.
- Find words and expressions which point to what the writer thinks.

Speak for yourself

1 Look at the three photos. What's your immediate reaction? Note down three words/phrases for each.

2 Describe the photos in as much detail as you can.

Reading

Between the lines

1 Quickly read the three articles. Match the photos to the stories.

2 Look at the headlines again and explain the word play in each. Turn to *p.109* if you need a clue.

3 Find evidence of the writers' opinions.

  1 Does the writer of the first article think these dolls are a good or a bad idea?

  2 How did the dogs, the owner, and the writer feel about the wedding?

  3 How many references to cars and driving can you find in the third article? What does the writer feel about the event?

My little cloney

To some people the idea might seem a little scary. To others, nothing could be cuter than a two-foot doll that's the *spitting image* of its owner. Parents send the company a personal profile and photograph of their child. A replica is made, and even the clothing is copied. 'I cried when I first opened the box because the doll was so much like my daughter,' said one satisfied customer. Others might find it in bad taste. *My Twinn* spokesman Dave Liggett says the dolls 'help kids and families feel good about themselves and appreciate how special and unique they are.' Psychologist Jenny Smith has a different point of view. 'This is a toy for adults', she says, 'to remind them of their children when they are not there. It's a good child – one who never has a dirty nose or a hair out of place.'

I pronounce you man and woof

'Dearly beloved, by the power invested in me by the state of California, I now pronounce you Mr and Mrs. You may now lick the bride', announced the minister at the end of the ceremony. And even if Tyson and Blossom were more interested in the bowl of dog biscuits at the reception than each other, the delight on their owners' faces was clearly enough to justify the expense. Blossom's owner, Charlene Brusha, a 45-year-old housewife from Beverly Hills said, 'They have lived together for seven years so we thought it was about time to make things official.' A wedding for two dogs causes hardly any surprises round here.

Rust in peace

Along life's road they were inseparable – one man and his car. Now, two months after his death, George Swanson has his final wish – to be buried in his cherished Chevrolet Corvette. He was cremated, and, after getting the green light from cemetery officials, his wife Caroline placed his ashes in the gleaming white coupé before it was lowered into a garage-sized grave. 'It's what he always wanted,' she said. George, a big wheel in the beer distribution trade, was determined to drive it into eternity with him. The cemetery has now changed its regulations to prevent cars being used as coffins.

spitting image exactly the same

The Daily Mail

ROSS

CATHY

EMMA

Listening
Instant opinions

1 In groups of three, **A** listen to Ross, **B** to Cathy, **C** to Emma. Write 'for' or 'against'.

	Ross	Cathy	Emma
My little cloney			
Man and woof			
Rust in peace			

2 Listen again. Note one reason why they felt that way. Tell your group.

English in use
Giving opinions

Stating your point of view

I think it's a _____ crazy.
As far as I'm c_____ ...
I'm sure _____ ...
I don't b_____ in ...

I think it's a w_____ of time.
In my o_____ ...
P_____ I think ...

Quoting someone else

A_____ to ...

Contradicting and reacting

Yes, b_____ ...
H_____ weird! H_____ awful!

W_____ a terrible idea!

Making similarities

It's l _____ ...

People often use emphatic stress to highlight the words which carry their opinions and emotions.

> I think they're <u>ab</u>solutely <u>gor</u>geous.

1 Complete the ways of giving opinions. Then check with the Tapescript on *pp.117/118.*

2 Listen and mark the stress. Then copy the intonation.
  1 It's like dogs having psychiatrists.
  2 I think it's absolutely crazy.
  3 As far as I'm concerned dogs are dogs and people are people.
  4 Personally I think they shouldn't be allowed.
  5 How weird!

3 Take turns to read and respond to these statements with the expressions above. Be as definite and as emphatic as possible!

People who eat meat are murderers.

Women are better drivers than men.

Astrology is an underrated science.

Men with beards have something to hide.

Every citizen should experience a period of military service.

Prisons these days are like holiday camps.

People should be free to smoke wherever they want.

The more I know people the better I like dogs.

Key word

thing

1 They think it's the thing to do.

2 He's been buried the way he wanted, that's the main thing.

3 The thing is, I could see it quickly becoming abused.

4 It's fine for a child to have a doll, but quite another thing for it to look exactly like her.

5 All things considered, it's not a good idea.

6 It's great to do your own thing.

7 My daughter's into this sort of thing.

1 Highlight the expressions with *thing* in **1** to **7**. Match them with meanings **a** to **g**.

- a having thought about all the facts ☐
- b it's completely different ☐
- c the most important ☐
- d similar activities ☐
- e fashionable ☐
- f the point is ☐
- g do as you please ☐

2 In pairs, take turns to respond with an expression with *thing*.

1 I'm going to have my eyebrows pierced. What do you think?

2 We had a good time even though the food was terrible and it rained.

3 Could I borrow your German dictionary this weekend?

4 Dad, you know we agreed I could go to the States? Well, I want to hitch-hike!

5   Do you think we should fly to Paris or take the train?

6 Would you like to go on an organized holiday this year?

7 Why does your brother play around with old motorbikes?

Speak out

For the sake of argument

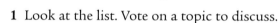

1 Look at the list. Vote on a topic to discuss.

- Cars should be banned from the centre of towns.
- Genetically-engineered food is a wonderful development.
- Smoking in public places should be banned.
- People who prefer animals to humans are mad.
- Children shouldn't be allowed to watch TV.

Think before you speak

- Use as many different ways as you can of giving opinions.
- Use emphatic stress to show how strongly you feel.
- Try to include at least one expression with *thing*.

2 Decide whether you personally feel positive or negative about the topic. List three points you'd like to make about it.

3 Form groups and discuss your opinions. Challenge and disagree as much as you can.

26 THE BIGGEST HOAX OF ALL?

In this lesson

- Revise and extend modal verbs to describe degrees of certainty.
- Look at how you feel about lies and deception.
- Practise following a discussion and making notes.

Speak for yourself

1 Read about how liars behave. How accurate do you think it is?

HOW TO SPOT A LIAR

People who lie ...
- often play with their collars or clothes.
- rub the side of their noses and cover their mouths.
- go red or laugh nervously.
- either look you in the eye too much, or else look away.

2 Quickly ask around the class. Who is the most truthful?

Do you think it's OK to ...?

- say someone looks nice when you think they look awful
- say 'I love you' when you don't mean it
- be inaccurate about your age or weight
- not be truthful about how much you earn
- say 'thank you' for a present you don't like
- say you look forward to seeing someone again when you don't
- tell children that Father Christmas is real

3 How important is the truth to you? Are you a good liar?

Listening
Real life or hoax?

1 Read the text and look at the photos. How much do you know about these events?

Armstrong steps from the capsule onto the moon.

The astronaut drives around in the moon buggy.

Splash down in the ocean.

ONE GIANT LEAP FOR AMERICA?

On July 20th 1969, Neil Armstrong satisfied one of mankind's deep, almost mystical ambitions. He stepped, for the first time in history, on ground that was not part of the Earth. He walked on the moon. On October 4th 1957 the Soviet Union had put a spacecraft, Sputnik, into orbit. This was followed by a series of Soviet firsts, and the Americans needed a boost to their confidence. On May 25th 1961 President Kennedy committed the country to putting a man on the moon before the decade was out. That man was Neil Armstrong.

The Sunday Times

2 Match the words and definitions.

space suit	radiation	atmosphere	gravity	launch

1. the gases surrounding a planet
2. send a rocket into space
3. clothing for astronauts
4. the force which attracts things to the earth
5. dangerous rays

3 You're going to hear a conversation about the 1969 moon landings. Listen to **Part A**. What does Martin think?

4 Listen to **Part B**. What evidence does Martin give for his argument?

Problem	Evidence
• the space suits	
• the space capsule	
• the photos taken from the moon	
• the dust from the moon buggy	

5 Listen to **Part C**. According to Martin:

1 What were the astronauts doing during the launch?

2 What was the reason for the hoax?

Degrees of certainty

Grammar revisited

1 Complete with *must, might, could,* or *can't*.

1 That _____ be the postman. He always comes at 8.00.

2 You _____ still be hungry after all that cake.

3 John said he _____ drop in after work if he can.

4 You've been working hard all day. You _____ be tired.

5 I'll check but I think she _____ be having a bath.

6 The sea _____ be warm enough; it's only April.

7 Answer the phone, Paul! It _____ be important.

8 You _____ be joking! I'm not going out now.

2 Check your answers in the Summary on *p.75*.

3 In pairs, make sentences about people you know.
Pierre *must* be tired. He was out very late last night.

Grammar plus

4 [○2] Listen and complete the sentences.

1 The astronauts _____ of radiation.

2 The stars _____ shone like headlights.

3 People _____ guessed.

4 The dust _____ much longer to fall.

5 The whole thing _____ in a studio.

5 Check with the Tapescript on *p.118*.

6 Listen again and copy the pronunciation of *have*.

---

would and *should*

• subject + *would have* + past participle
Sue would have helped you.
(she didn't help because she wasn't asked)

• subject + *should have* + past participle
Mike should have won that game.
(he didn't win but was expected to)

---

7 Read the text. Do you think it's true, or a hoax?

German scientists have discovered that mummies in European museums contain large amounts of cocaine and nicotine. Critics say that this ¹_____ (not be) true, as both drugs were unavailable in Egypt until the discovery of the Americas at the end of the 15th century, so it's impossible that these tests ²_____ (find) traces of the drugs. One theory is that archaeologists ³_____ (contaminate) them by smoking during their examinations. However, most scientists agree that this ⁴_____ (not be) true as the levels of nicotine in the mummies are far too high. Another explanation is that the Egyptian priests ⁵_____ (wrap) the bodies in a kind of tobacco which grew in the Nile Delta. They obviously ⁶_____ (not know) that it would be bad for the health of their masters in the afterlife!

The cocaine is more of a problem, but it is now widely accepted that there ⁷_____ (be) trade between west Africa and central America where the coca leaf grows. In this way, leaves ⁸_____ (find) their way to Egypt where they ⁹_____ (use) in medicines. It also explains how the Aztecs ¹⁰_____ (obtain) the know-how for their own pyramids. This offends some Latin American archaeologists who say their pyramids are so different that they ¹¹_____ (evolve) independently. The scientists ¹²_____ (not be) sure until further tests have been carried out.

8 Complete the text. Use modal verbs and the verbs in brackets.

9 Check the forms of *must, might, could,* and *can't* in the Summary on *p.75*.

Against the clock!

Set a time limit

10 In pairs, reply to these questions.

1 Who is that at the door? I'm not expecting anyone.
2 Where do you think you left your keys?
3 What would our ancestors have thought about the way we live nowadays?
4 Whose is that bag over there?
5 Do you know which language those two are speaking?
6 I asked for two kilos of peaches. Why are there only four in the bag?
7 I wonder why that plant has died.
8 David has gone straight to bed. Why do you think he is so tired?
9 Who do you think painted that marvellous picture?
10 Why are you feeling ill? Did you eat something strange?
11 Do you have any idea what the time is?
12 Why do you think he never phoned back? I left three messages.

Speak out
What happened?

1 In groups, choose one of the pictures. Decide what happened.

Think before you speak

- Use the modal verbs you have studied.
- Use weak forms and contractions where appropriate.

2 With a partner from another group, tell your version of the story.

SUMMARY

Probability and certainty

Present form

modal verb + infinitive / progressive infinitive
She **might come** / she **might be coming**.

Past form

modal verb + *have* + past participle
She **must have arrived** last night.

Use

- *must* when you are almost completely sure that something is true.
- *might / could / may* when you are not sure whether something is true or not.
- *can't* when you are almost completely sure that something isn't true.

27
IT'S MY LIFE

In this lesson

- Look at controversial topics and discuss responsibility.
- Practise ways of criticizing and blaming.
- Evaluate opinions from a text.

Speak for yourself

1 Which would you choose?
- to do a job you enjoy for a poor salary, or a well-paid job you hate
- to have a small but convenient flat, or a large house and travel a long way every day
- to have a new house and an old car, or a new car and an old house
- to be brilliant at one thing, or average at lots of things
- to tell a lie or to betray a friend

2 Think of a difficult decision you've had to make. What did you decide to do? Did you get advice or pressure from family / friends?

Reading
Looking for opinions

1 Read the text. What do the following refer to?

16	A-level	£6,500	New York	$1,000,000
44	Milan and Paris	engineering	unreal	

Model pupil who prefers it at school

SHE looks like any other schoolgirl, fresh-faced and full of life. Sarah Thomas is looking forward to the challenge of her new A-level course. But unlike her schoolfriends, 16-year-old Sarah is not spending half-term resting. Instead, she is earning £6,500 a day as a catwalk model in New York.

Sarah has been told that she could be Britain's new supermodel, earning a million dollars in the next year. Her father Peter, 44, wants her to give up school to model full-time. But Sarah, who has taken part in shows alongside top models, wants to prove that she has brains as well as beauty. She is determined to carry on with her education.

She has turned down invitations to star at shows in Milan and Paris later this autumn in order to concentrate on her studies. After school she plans to take a year off to model full-time before going to university to get a degree in engineering or architecture.

Sarah says, 'My dad thinks I should take the opportunity now. But at the moment, school comes first. I don't want to get too involved in the fashion world. Modelling is fun but the lifestyle is a little unreal. I don't want to have nothing else to fall back on when I can't model any more.'

The Express

Effective reading

When you are reading about controversial events:

- Look for all the different opinions expressed in the text.
- Compare them with your own. Who do you agree with most?

2 Think about how the following people might feel.
- Sarah
- the model agency
- Sarah's father
- Sarah's teacher

3 What would you do in Sarah's situation?

Vocabulary
Verbs in context

1 Find verbs in the text which mean ...

    1 to await with excitement.   **4** to continue.

    2 to stop doing.   **5** to refuse an offer.

    3 to participate.   **6** to use for support when in difficulty.

2 Which verbs can be separated by their object?

3 Make true sentences using the six verbs.

Listening
A controversial topic

1 Listen to Gerry and Martine discussing Sarah's story. Whose opinions are these? Write Gerry (G), or Martine (M).

    1 Sarah should have taken up a modelling career. ☐

    2 It's good that she doesn't care about her looks. ☐

    3 She has an opportunity to make a lot of money. ☐

    4 She should have earned the money for her family. ☐

    5 Her family would exploit her. ☐

    6 Her dad shouldn't have talked to the newspapers. ☐

    7 Her dad didn't want her to miss a great opportunity. ☐

    8 Sarah will regret her decision later on. ☐

2 Listen and repeat. Tick the opinions you agree with.

    1 She _____ made millions.

    2 He _____ felt sick.

    3 He _____ spoken to them.

    4 I _____ a lot if I hadn't stayed at school.

3 Write the missing words in full.

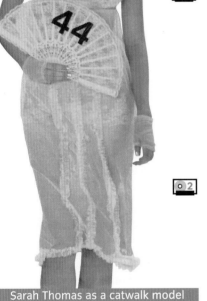

Sarah Thomas as a catwalk model

English in use
Criticizing and blaming

Implying blame

Use forms of *should*, *ought to*, and *could* to criticize past actions.

    She should have taken her chance.

    She ought to have done it for her family.

    She could have made millions.

Expressions with *blame* and *fault* show strong criticism.

    You blame **someone** for doing **something**.

    I blame him for talking to the newspapers.

    It's someone's **fault** for doing **something**.

    It's his fault for attracting all this interest.

It's better to use these expressions <u>about</u> someone or something. To say them directly to someone is very critical and sounds rude.

Showing impatience

We use *on earth* to show impatience or strong surprise.

Why on earth didn't she take it?   What on earth for?

1 Complete with a question word.

1 _____ on earth have you been? It's two o'clock in the morning.

2 _____ on earth have you done to my CD player? It doesn't work any more.

3 _____ on earth is that at the door? We're not expecting visitors.

4 We've missed the last bus. _____ on earth are we going to get home?

5 She's really upset. _____ on earth did you tell her the truth?

2 Listen and copy the intonation.

3 In pairs, **A** turn to *p.109*, **B** to *p.111* and roleplay.

Speak out
Who's responsible?

1 Read the story. Number the pictures in the right order.

the story of
Stephanie H.

Stephanie H. lived in a village in the English countryside where she worked in a bookshop. She was deeply in love with her boyfriend Raymond, a dreamy poet and writer. However, Raymond suddenly ended their relationship. A few months later she met and married Cedric, a successful businessman, and went to live in his huge house in the countryside. The house was close to a hospital for dangerous criminals. One winter's morning, as Cedric was about to drive to London on business, Stephanie heard on the radio that a dangerous madman had escaped from the hospital. She begged Cedric to take her with him but he said it was not possible. She was scared of being alone so she drove to the village bookshop where, by chance, she met Raymond. They had dinner at his place, where Stephanie spent the night on the sofa. The following morning her car wouldn't start but Raymond refused to give her a lift because he was afraid of what Cedric would do if he saw them together. Stephanie was furious and caught a taxi. She discussed the escaped madman with the taxi driver. At the crossroads to her home she realized she had left her keys and money at Raymond's house. When she told the driver he made her get out of the car. 'No money, no ride', he said. As she turned up the path the madman jumped from behind a tree and killed her.

Think before you speak

- Use forms of *should, could,* and *ought to*.
- Use expressions with *fault* and *blame*.
- Use contractions where appropriate.

2 Who do you think was responsible for Stephanie's death? Rank the characters from 1 (most responsible) to 5 (least responsible).

☐ Stephanie   ☐ the madman   ☐ the taxi driver
☐ Cedric   ☐ Raymond

3 Discuss your order in groups. Vote on the most/least responsible.

4 Turn to *p.110*. Read the interpretation of your order. What do you think?

28
LIGHTING A CANDLE

In this lesson

- Extend your vocabulary to do with current affairs.
- Look at how news headlines work.
- Focus on the work of an international charity.

a — The manager of your national football team has resigned following arguments with top players.

b — *Two aid workers from your country have been taken hostage in Africa.*

c — A café in a small country village has sold three winning lottery tickets in the last three months.

Headlines

Short, dramatic words are generally chosen for headlines. Compare:

> SOCCER + ROW + BOSS + QUITS (= 18 letters)
> Football + argument + manager + resigns (= 30 letters)

The present simple is often used in place of the past or the present perfect. The infinitive is used to express the future.

> SOCCER BOSS QUITS = a football manager has resigned
> NEW PLANT TO OPEN = a new factory is going to open

Speak for yourself

1 Think about the last news bulletin you heard. How much of it was devoted to ...?

| disasters | politics | sport | business | the economy | good news |

2 Consider the following stories for a five-minute news broadcast.
  1 Choose which stories to include, and the running order.
  2 Decide how long you would give to each.

d — A painting which won the £10,000 first prize in a modern art competition was in fact painted by a four-year-old child.

e — *A new factory providing 2,000 jobs is going to be opened in an area of high unemployment.*

f — A child suffering from leukaemia is miraculously cured at a holy place in your country.

g — Two firemen have been killed in an explosion at an oil refinery.

h — A blind woman has climbed to the top of Mount Everest.

Vocabulary

In the news

1 Which of the news stories above do these headlines go with?
  1 On top of the world ☐   3 Soccer row boss quits ☐
  2 Touched by God ☐   4 New plant to open ☐

2 Match the headline words in **A** with a synonym in **B**.

A			B		
fury	urge	wed	marry	dismiss	explosion
drama	blast	back	anger	encourage	support
split	sack		excitement	disagreement	

3 Expand the stories behind these headlines.
  1 CHURCH LEADER URGES SINGLE MUMS TO WED
  2 MINISTER SACKED AFTER CABINET SPLIT
  3 FURY AT REFINERY BLAST DEATHS
  4 DRAMA AS JUDGE BACKS STRIKERS

4 **Against the clock!** Make nouns from these adjectives and mark the word stress in two minutes.
  1 furious   3 afraid   5 unemployed   7 homeless
  2 miserable 4 cruel   6 corrupt   8 poor

HANDICAP INTERNATIONAL

One of the biggest international news stories of recent years has been the problems caused by land mines. More than ever before, *civilians* are the greatest victims of war. *Refugees* are forced to *flee* their homes and *seek* safety elsewhere. Then, on returning home, they discover that the countryside they once farmed has hidden minefields. Clearing these mines will take many years and in the meantime there are thousands of *casualties* in need of urgent help. 'Handicap International' is a charity which helps the *victims* of land mines by supplying medical help and *equipment* such as *crutches* and *artificial limbs* for people who have been disabled by these terrible *weapons*.

Listening
Words in context

1 Read about the work of 'Handicap International'. Would you give money to this sort of charity?

2 Which of the words in *italics* in the text means ...?

  1 to run away
  2 tools / material
  3 a soldier's 'tools'
  4 ordinary citizens
  5 injured people

  6 something to help you to walk
  7 to look for
  8 people forced to leave a war zone
  9 substitute arms and legs
  10 people who suffer at the hands of others

3 Joelle Chivers is talking about the problems charities face. Listen to **Part 1**. Change one word to correct sentences 1 to 5.
  1 Charities hate to spend money on advertising.
  2 There's so much complication now between different organizations.
  3 We all hate giving money to help world politics ...
  4 ... half of it is going to rich American companies.
  5 Charities have to build a bland name like any other business.

4 Listen to **Part 2**. Explain the significance of ...

| begging letters | unopened | close to home | indifferent |

5 Listen to **Part 3**. How did Handicap International ...?
  1 encourage people to open their letters
  2 get across the importance of the work they do

Speak out
Problem circles

1 Work in small groups.
  1 Individually, write three important problems in each circle.
  2 Choose one circle and tell your group more about it.
  3 Make a group drawing of the problem circles. Agree on three problems to put in each circle.

2 Your government has decided to produce a set of stamps to recognize people who have worked for good causes locally or internationally. Which figures would you choose to appear in your set of stamps? Agree on one for each circle.

your town

your country

the world

Think before you speak
• Use as much of the vocabulary to do with news and world affairs as you can.
• Practise using noun forms from adjectives.
• Use the correct word stress.

29 RUMOURS

In this lesson

- Focus on the rights and wrongs of gossiping.
- Look at expressions / intonation for gossiping.
- Practise listening to and passing on rumours.

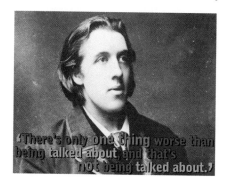

'There's only one thing worse than being talked about, and that's not being talked about.'

Speak for yourself

1 Read the dictionary definitions. Give another example of each word.

gossip *n* Casual talk about the private lives of other people. *She's too fond of idle gossip.*

rumour *n* News or information that many people are talking about but may not be true. *There are a lot of rumours going round about the factory closing.*

scandal *n* Behaviour or a situation that shocks people. *There has been another financial scandal involving a bank in London.*

2 Who do you think gossip more, men or women?

3 Which magazines and newspapers that you know are famous for public 'gossip'?

1 What sort of people do they write about?

2 How much of what you read do you think is true?

3 How fair is it to expose the private lives of public people? Give examples.

Listening
Headhunting

1 Describe the people in the photos. What do you think they're like?

A

Hello, Hugh, do you remember me? Trevor Watson, from Johnson's.

Trevor, of course. So what brings you to Birmingham?

B

C

2 Sandra and Roger both work at 'Johnson's', a business based in London. They are having a quick break by the coffee machine. Listen to **Part 1**.

1 What's Sandra's piece of gossip?
2 What conclusions does she draw? Do you think they're correct?

3 Roger is phoning his friend Alex. Listen to **Part 2**.

1 What does Roger add to Sandra's gossip?
2 What conclusion does Alex draw?

4 What do you think might happen as a result?

English in use
How to gossip

1 Complete the phrases below. Check with the Tapescript on *pp.118/119*.

Passing on gossip

When people gossip they usually follow a particular pattern.

* They signal that they've got some gossip.
  You'll never _____ .
* They often ask the other person to keep the gossip secret.
  Promise you _____ .
* They don't give all the information at once; instead, they build the gossip up.
  He was with Hugh Black from ABC … And they were deep in conversation.

Listening to gossip

When people listen to gossip they respond in a particular way too.

* They signal that they are ready to listen, and sound interested.
  No, go on …
* They promise secrecy.
  I won't _____ .
* They keep the gossip going by responding to each new piece of information.
  What can it mean? … And did Trevor see you?
* They make comments to show interest and surprise.
  I don't _____ it! How _____ ! Well, well!

Gossipers use a wide voice range to show interest and surprise.

2 Find more examples of passing on and listening to gossip from the two conversations.

3 When would you use these expressions?

I won't tell a soul …

I don't like to spread gossip but …

Go on! I'm all ears.

Promise you won't tell a soul?

My lips are sealed

4 Listen to these extracts and mark the stress. Then copy the intonation.

1 You'll never guess who I saw.
2 Promise you won't tell anyone?
3 I won't breathe a word.
4 No, really?
5 Well, well!
6 I heard something that might interest you.
7 This is in the strictest confidence.
8 My lips are sealed.

Speak out
Rumours

1 Think of a rumour of your own. (Do <u>not</u> create any rumours about people in your class!) Base it around ...
- famous people.
- work issues.
- national or international news.

2 Make sure you can answer the following.
- How did you find out about it?
- Who is involved?
- What do you think might happen?

3 Exchange rumours with other members of your class. Each time your teacher tells you to move on, spread the gossip you have heard, adding a detail of your own.

Think before you speak
- Remember to signal that you've got some gossip or are ready to hear about it.
- Respond with interest/surprise using a wide voice range.
- Try to build the gossip up, or keep it going with questions.

In this lesson

- Revise and extend the language of hypothesizing.
- Look at differences between the sexes.
- Practise discussing alternative lives and lifestyles.

Speak for yourself

1 Would you prefer to have been born the opposite sex? Why (not)?

2 Read this situation. What would you do? Discuss your answers.

- A 6-year-old boy asks you to buy him a doll for his birthday.
- A friend who told you she was expecting a boy has, in fact, had a girl. You have already bought a blue sleepsuit for the baby.

3 Do you think boys and girls are ...?
- born with different characteristics
- made to behave differently by parents / society
- basically the same; it depends on their personality

Reading
Making notes

1 Change one letter to correct the verbs in **bold**. Find the verbs in the texts.
1 I **wondered** around the shop looking at the clothes.
2 He **flitted** outrageously with the barmaid.
3 Youths **room** the streets at night looking for trouble.
4 She offered to **hand up** my coat on the hook.
5 His voice broke and he started to **share** when he was fourteen.

2 Read about a husband and wife who swapped roles for a week. In pairs, **A** read Text A, **B** read Text B. Make notes about your text.
- dressing
- travelling
- going out
- pleasant experiences
- unpleasant experiences

3 Tell your partner about your text using the notes you made.

Text A

Monday Getting dressed as a woman is so complicated! It takes 45 minutes just to shave my legs. I've noticed that women smile more in general – and when I don't smile, my face looks too masculine.
Tuesday I go shopping. A street trader tries to sell me something. When I say, 'No, thank you,' he replies, 'Ooh, sexy voice!' Suddenly I feel angry that a simple exchange of remarks has to be made into something sexual. I take the train home during rush hour. A man sits down next to me with his legs apart, crowding me.
Wednesday Major fashion crisis! My outfit doesn't feel right. I realize that being a woman means being continually noticed and assessed. As I stand outside a shop waiting for a friend, an older man looks me up and down. I feel uncomfortable, and try to avoid looking at him.
Simon as Sheila
Thursday I have a lunch date with my friend Isobel. I'm feeling pretty good until I find myself faced with groups of businessmen roaming the streets.
Friday In the evening we go to a club. The place is packed. I feel very self-conscious again. I notice I expect my partner to do everything for me – get my drinks, hang up my coat.

Text B

Monday How much easier it is to be a man! No hair curling, no mascara. I try to sit like a man, with my legs apart. I'm really taking up space, and it feels great. I go to a cocktail party. I'm very careful to lower my voice. I realize I'm much more animated than the other men around me. Gradually, I try to act more like they do.
Tuesday At the bank we watch out carefully for any strange looks. Again, no reaction. Then it's off to lunch. I take huge, macho bites of my chicken, and nearly choke. I meet my friend Rick in a small pub. He flirts with the barmaid. He obviously feels it's OK to flirt in front of a man.
Wednesday Waiting for my partner to get ready. 'She's' driving me crazy! I'm wearing jeans and a shirt.
Thursday I feel safe enough to sleep on the train – I've never done that before. I go into a tool shop. Usually the men follow me, assuming I wouldn't know a hammer from a saw. Today they let me wander around.
Sheila as Simon
Friday After dinner we go to a club. I push through the crowd, leading the way. My last day as a man. I'll miss the ease of getting dressed and the extra confidence. At the same time, I can't wait to be a woman again.

Woman's Journal

Listening
Alternatives

🔘1　1　Listen to three people talking about who / what they would like to have been. Write a name under each picture.

RON	CARMEN	IAN

2　Listen again. Why did they choose these things? What do we find out about their personalities?

3　Who / what would you like to have been?

Hypothesizing

Grammar revisited

1 Complete the conditional sentences.

1　If I had two weeks' holiday …
2　If the weather is good at the weekend …
3　If I hadn't eaten breakfast this morning …
4　If I get my bonus at work …
5　If I spoke perfect English …
6　If I hadn't worked so hard yesterday …
7　If I don't pass this exam …
8　If I could go to any country …

2 Check the forms you used in the Summary on *p.86*.

3 Complete the sentences. Use the verbs in brackets.

1　The party was really good. If you _____ (come) you _____ (enjoy) yourself.
2　Her life _____ (be) easier if she _____ (have) a car but she can't afford one.
3　If she _____ (know) about his strange habits, she _____ (never marry) him.
4　I'm not sure about this. What do you think you _____ (do) if you _____ (be) in my position?
5　I _____ (let) you use my car if you _____ (promise) to bring it back this afternoon.
6　Thanks for your help yesterday. I don't know what I _____ (do) if you _____ (not be) there.

Grammar plus

4 Complete these sentences.

1　I wish I _____ remember people's names. It's so embarrassing!
2　I wish I _____ not lent Simon that money. I'm sure I'll never see it again.

3　I wish Jenny _____ not talk about her wedding so much. It's really annoying!
4　I wish I _____ a bit taller. This dress would look so much better.

5 What would these people say? Use *wish*.

1　Jenny can't sleep because she ate a very spicy meal late in the evening.
2　Paul can't stop thinking about his ex-girlfriend.
3　Malcolm lost his temper with Barbara and now regrets it.
4　Roger is jealous of his friend's dancing ability.
5　Mary finds Martin's habit of singing in the shower really irritating.
6　Rachel wants to go on holiday with her friends but can't get the time off work.

6 Find examples of hypothesizing in the Tapescript on *p.119*. Decide why each form is used.

7 🔘2 Listen and copy the intonation. How do you pronounce *have*?

Forms of *wish*

- Use *wish* + past simple to express regrets about the present / hopes for the future.
  I wish I had a flat of my own. (I don't have a flat but I would like one)

- Use *wish* + *could* + base form to express lack of ability or possibility.
  I wish I could play tennis better. (I can't play tennis but I would like to be able to)

- Use *wish* + past perfect to express regrets about the past which can't be changed.
  I wish I hadn't gone to bed so late last night. (I went to bed late last night and now I'm tired)

- Use *wish* + *would* + base form to express irritation.
  I wish he wouldn't smoke in the office.
  I wish you would hurry up!

Set a time limit

8 In small groups, look at the picture story. How many things went wrong during the evening?

9 Decide what comments the couple might have made at the end of the evening. Write as many sentences as you can.

If it hadn't rained so hard I wouldn't have caught a cold.

I wish I had brought my umbrella.

Speak out
Second chances

I did it my way...

Think before you speak

- Try to use a variety of conditional forms accurately.
- Include sentences with *wish*.
- Use weak forms and contractions correctly.

1 Do you have any regrets about your own upbringing, school days, studies, and choice of career?

- Think of something you wish you had done differently.
- What would you have done instead?
- What do you think would have happened if you had made different choices?

2 Draw an alternative 'road of life' for yourself. Explain it to your group.

SUMMARY
Conditional forms

First conditional

- If + simple present + *will / won't* + base form
  If he studies hard, he'll pass his exams.
  (it is possible that he will study hard and therefore possible he will pass)

Second conditional

- If + past simple + *would(n't)* + base form
  If I worked all day, I would finish this report.
  (it is improbable that I will work all day and therefore unlikely that I will finish the report)

Third conditional

- If + past perfect + *would(n't) have* + past participle
  If I had gone to that party, I would have met Michael.
  (I didn't go to the party and therefore didn't meet Michael and now I regret it)

Mixed conditional

- If + past perfect + *would(n't)* + base form
  If I hadn't had such a big lunch, I wouldn't be so sleepy now.
  (I ate too much for lunch and am sleepy now)

In this lesson

- Look at techniques for effective communication.
- Focus on how other people see us.
- Practise reading between the lines.

Speak for yourself

1 Read about the Johari Window. What do the following represent?

the house	room 1	room 2	room 3	room 4

2 What do you think of this technique?

    a fascinating and useful

    b intriguing but not really useful

    c complete rubbish

The Johari Window is a technique for describing someone's personality. The house represents us, each of us. Other people can look in through Window A, but we can only see through Window B. Room 1 is common knowledge; it is the part of us which we see and others see. But there are three other rooms. There is room 2, the aspect of us which others see but which we are not aware of, and there is room 4, our private space, which we know but keep from others because we are shy or just private. Finally there is the mysterious room 3, the unconscious or subconscious bit of us which is seen by neither ourselves nor outsiders.

Charles Handy

Reading
Between the lines

1 Read about Vicky. Match a name from below to these opinions of her.

- hard-working and calm
- untidy and impatient
- sporty and insensitive
- romantic and talkative

2 How close is her image of herself to the way other people see her?

Vicky 24, teacher
Fun-loving, adventurous brunette, passionate about basketball and motorbikes, looking for my very own, tall, handsome sportsman to take me for a spin.

Sam 23, student
Vicky's younger sister
Whirlwind basketball fan wants a sporty tolerant man to organize her. Sense of humour and a thick skin essential. Men who enjoy cosy nights in need not apply.

Lee 25, mechanic
Vicky's first serious boyfriend
Loyal, honest, and forgiving 24-year-old looking for love from exciting, jealousy-free man tolerant of endless chatter.

Terry 52
Vicky's Mum
Attractive but messy 24-year-old needs non-demanding man to idolize her. Must be patient and tolerant because she's not!

Joanna 27
a fellow teacher
Quiet, committed professional, good with children, interested in meeting sports fan for watching and playing.

Best magazine

1 John tends to ramble when he's explaining things. I find myself switching off after a few minutes, and that means I miss a lot of what he says.

2 Errol always appears to listen but I'm not sure if he's really taking in what I say. He rarely says anything back to me that shows he understands the point I'm making. It can be like talking to a brick wall.

3 Marcus asks too many questions. It's like being interrogated by a detective rather than having a conversation.

4 Gloria barges straight in and starts a conversation without considering whether it's a good time for me to talk. I feel under terrible pressure because I don't want to be rude. But because I've got other things on my mind, I don't really pay that much attention to her.

Talk Works

3 Check back in the text. Find words or expressions which mean ...

1 very energetic
2 able to put up with a lot
3 not sensitive to criticism
4 empty talk
5 to worship like a god
6 fully engaged in one's work

4 Look again at the text. Decide what each person really thinks of her.
1 Give her a score out of ten from each person (e.g. 7 out of 10).
2 What clues in the text helped you to understand their opinions?

5 Write an anonymous profile of your own personality. Read other people's paragraphs and guess who they are.

Listening
Conversational reputations

1 Match 'conversational profiles' 1 to 4 to the four descriptions below.
- he/she interrupts inconsiderately ☐
- he/she carries out an interrogation ☐
- he/she talks without a clear direction ☐
- he/she doesn't concentrate during a conversation ☐

2 Explain these words/expressions.

ramble	switch off	take in	barge in	pay attention

3 Do the profiles remind you of anyone you know? Do you do any of these things?

4 Listen to four conversations. Match them to the speakers. What are they talking about?

Speaker	Conversation	Topic
John		
Errol		
Marcus		
Gloria		

English in use
Making conversation

 1 Listen to the speakers using better conversational techniques.
1 How does Marcus make his questions sound less abrupt?
2 How does Gloria make her request sound more considerate?
3 How does John make his directions clearer and more organized?
4 How does Errol show he's really listening?

2 Look at the Tapescript on *p.119*. Find more examples of the following.

Conversational techniques

You can make a series of questions less abrupt by adding comments, softeners, and by using indirect questions. Compare:

> Many people there?
> Oh right, and I expect it must have been quite crowded?

A good technique is to empathize with the other person's story, i.e. put yourself in their position.

> So it must have been hard to get home?

You can persuade someone to talk more easily, even if they are busy, by using polite requests and flattering them.

> I was wondering if you could ...?

When you are asked for information, try not to get distracted from what you are explaining. Add any extra comments after you've finished.

> By the way ...

You can show you're listening by reformulating what the other person says, and by acknowledging the other person's point of view.

> So you think ...
> I hear what you're saying ...

 3 Listen and copy the intonation.

4 In pairs, roleplay these situations.

1 **A** You think the latest fashions are ridiculous.
B Acknowledge how **A** feels and then give an alternative opinion.

2 **A** You would like to borrow **B**'s dictionary this weekend. Make a tentative request.
B Say it's OK.

3 **A** Tell **B** that your flat was burgled while you were away on holiday.
B Empathize, and make a comment to comfort **A**.

4 **A** Ask if **B** would be willing to swap holiday dates with you.
B Reformulate what **A** says and continue.

Speak out
Effective communication

1 You have to organize an evening's entertainment for a group of about fifty people. Individually, think of ...
- a theme for the evening.
- the kind of food you will have.
- the kind of music there will be.
- a show or another form of entertainment.

2 **A** discuss your ideas with a partner. Ask for their opinion. **B** listen, and make suggestions of your own.

3 Agree on a final programme for the evening.

Think before you speak
- Acknowledge the other person's point of view even if you don't agree with them.
- Show you are listening by reformulating what the other person says.
- Ask questions about their ideas without being abrupt.

Speak for yourself

1 Look at these dictionary definitions describing people in business. Which ones have a negative connotation?

an entrepreneur a person who starts or organizes a commercial enterprise esp. one involving financial risk.

a high-flyer an ambitious and potentially very successful person.

a wheeler-dealer (*infml*) a person who is skilled at making business deals, often involving large amounts of money.

a whizz-kid (*infml esp. US*) a (young) person who is highly skilled in a particular area.

a yuppie (also *yuppy*) (*infml*) a young urban professional person who earns a lot of money in a city job and is ambitious.

2 In groups, think of people who are good examples of these.

Reading
Words in context

a willingness to take risks
financial knowledge
qualifications
ability to learn fast
optimism
ambition
self-belief
experience
modesty
luck
ability to innovate
ability to work hard
ability to identify opportunities

1 How important are the qualities in the circle for successful entrepreneurs? Give a mark out of ten for each.

2 Quickly read the text. What happened after each of these key words/phrases?
- When (they) came to London …
- Even though …
- Soon …
- They went on to …
- Within a couple of years …
- In the end …

3 Which factors from ex.1 contributed to the Svensons' success?

There are millions of people in big cities who seem to ¹ *live on* coffee, adrenaline, and little else. When Ally and Scott Svenson came to London from Seattle, they spent time ² *looking for* the perfect cup of coffee they had been used to back home. Even though they ³ *came across* the occasional Italian coffee shop in Soho, they soon realized that excellent coffee in clean coffee houses was generally unavailable. Soon they ⁴ *came up with* the idea of opening up their own Seattle-style coffee shop. Ally had a job in publishing but she ⁵ *gave it up* to work full-time in their first coffee shop in London's trendy Covent Garden. They ⁶ *went on to* open two more shops in their first year. Within a couple of years they had ⁷ *turned it into* a multi-million pound business. In the end, 'Starbuck Coffee', the chain which had provided their original inspiration back in Seattle, made them an offer they couldn't ⁸ *turn down*, and they allowed themselves to be ⁹ *taken over* by the US giant. They didn't ¹⁰ *give the business away* however, instead selling it for £49 million. Not bad for three years' work.

The Independent on Sunday

Vocabulary
Multi-word verbs

find by chance	stop doing
refuse	transform
try to find	proceed
assume control	think of
give something for nothing	
survive on	

1 Replace multi-word verbs 1 to 10 from the text on *p.90* with the definitions from the box.

2 Put the multi-word verbs in **1** to **4** under the correct heading.

INTRANSITIVE	SEPARABLE	INSEPARABLE	THREE-PART

1 They **came across** the occasional Italian coffee shop in Soho.
2 They **came up with** the idea of opening their own coffee shop.
3 She **gave it up** to work full-time in their first coffee shop.
4 They **went on to** open two more shops in their first year.

Recording multi-word verbs

- Write down new multi-word verbs as you come across them.
- Record multi-word verbs by topic.
  Relationships: go out with, get on with …
  Health: go down with, pass out, come to …
- Write a definition and an example sentence for context. (Show if the verb and particle can be separated.)
  turn into = transform
  She turned her dream into reality.

Listening
Follow your dream

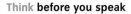 **1** Listen to the story of Leslie Scott, the inventor of a game called *Jenga*. What do these numbers refer to?

54	20	1,000	30	41	1991	1993	3,000,000

2 What similarities are there between Leslie Scott and the Svensons?

 3 **Against the clock!** In teams, turn to the Tapescript on *p.119*. See how many of the multi-word verbs in **bold** you know, or can guess from context in five minutes. Record any new ones.

Speak out
Success is sweet

1 In pairs, tell the story of 'Jemima's Jams'. Look at the first two pictures. **A** describe what's happening in Picture 1, **B** describe Picture 2.

2 **A** turn to *p.110*, **B** to *p.112*. Describe your pictures to each other, and work out the story between you.

3 When you have finished, compare with another pair. Are your stories the same?

Think before you speak

- Include at least five multi-word verbs in your story.
- Think about what type of multi-word verbs they are and use them accurately.
- Include some of the vocabulary of success.

PRACTICE

01

1 Match the statements with the responses.

1 I can't stand doing the ironing.   **a** Neither would we.
2 I really should be going now.   **b** That's funny, so did we.
3 We mustn't leave too late.   **c** Neither can I.
4 I'd rather take a taxi.   **d** Neither should you!
5 We didn't really enjoy the film.   **e** So should I.
6 You shouldn't drink so much.   **f** Neither must we.
7 They'd never buy a foreign car.   **g** So would I.
8 They had terrible weather.   **h** Neither did Susie.

2 Test your memory for 'party talk' Write the words in
the correct order.

1 is Mandy this Carrington. *This is Mandy Carrington.*
2 to there would is you meet someone I like.
3 wine you would a of glass like?
4 brings what so Paris you to?
5 Christina ages been it has!
6 a shame what oh!
7 excuse hope you I will me.
8 time the is that? really I going be must.
9 lovely you it has see to been.
10 have wonderful I a time had.
11 I together get can hope soon we.

02

3 Underline the correct verb form.

George   Is there anything interesting in that magazine?
Maisie   Yes, I ¹**have read/have been reading** about a man
         who collects spiders. He's got about seventy.
George   How long ²**has he been collecting/has he collected**
         them?
Maisie   I think he ³**keeps them/has been keeping them** for
         seven years. Yes, he ⁴**started/has started** seven years
         ago.

George   Why ⁵**has he been choosing/did he choose** this
         hobby?
Maisie   Because he ⁶**has wanted/wanted** to get over a fear
         of spiders.
George   ⁷**Have the spiders ever escaped?/Did the spiders ever**
         escape?
Maisie   No, he ⁸**was/has been** lucky.
George   And ⁹**has a spider ever bitten/did a spider ever bite**
         him?
Maisie   No, he ¹⁰**hasn't been bitten/wasn't bitten** yet.
George   Lucky guy! And only last week a bee ¹¹**has stung/**
         stung me!
Maisie   Look at this one. It's the biggest one I ¹²**have ever**
         seen/ever saw.

4 Complete the text. Use the verb in brackets.

And finally this evening, news ¹ *has just come in*
(just/come in) that a chamber-maid ² _____ (find)
a metre-long crocodile under the bed of a hotel in central
Paris this morning. Fortunately, experts from the local zoo
³ _____ (catch) the creature after a short hunt. This
is not the first time this ⁴ _____ (happen); a similar
event ⁵ _____ (occur) last week in another hotel in
the same area, but even though experts ⁶ _____
(search) for this one for days they ⁷ _____ (not find)
it yet. Customs officials claim that over the past few years
importers ⁸ _____ (smuggle) a large number of live
crocodiles into the country. A few years ago in New York
there ⁹ _____ (be) a fashion for buying pet alligators
which their owners ¹⁰ _____ (release) when they got
too big. Ever since there ¹¹ _____ (be) rumours of
giant alligators roaming the sewers of the city. ■

03

5 Complete the multi-word verbs to do with relationships.

1 Now you're 30 you should _settle_ **down** and start a family.
2 Can we _____ her **up** with Melanie's brother?
3 Have you heard? Chuck and Zoe have _____ **up**.
4 We've _____ **off** the wedding until next spring.
5 I _____ **into** Sylvie at the supermarket.
6 The film didn't _____ **up to** my expectations.
7 My 13-year-old has started _____ **out with** boys!
8 Sandra _____ me **out** the first time we met.
9 He's always _____ **on well with** his in-laws.
10 I don't want to _____ **into** marriage yet.

6 Rewrite the sentences using the KEY words.

1 He was expecting her to leave.   SURPRISED
   He wasn't surprised when she left.
2 It's not a good idea for people to marry too young.   SHOULDN'T
3 The news of their engagement was a surprise to me.   AMAZED
4 It was the best thing for them in my opinion.   PERSONALLY
5 Paul and Miriam are a good example.   TAKE
6 I was shocked when I heard that they had split up.   BELIEVE
7 It's time for you to think about your future.   OUGHT

04

7 ⏱ **Five-minute brainstorm** Write words / expressions.

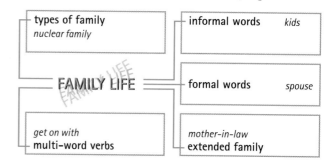

8 **Word challenge** Complete the words. Match the clues. Find the mystery word. Check on *p.13.*

```
      S  I           E
 R E  L              E  S
      S  U              D  D  Y
 B A                    R
                  H  E  R
         P           E  R
      S  I  B        G  S
 S P  I
      D  E  P     A  N  T  S
      D
```

people you are responsible for
opposite of *mother*
people in your family
unmarried man
rich older lover
formal *brothers / sisters*
informal *father*
unmarried
unmarried woman
the person you have a close relationship with

Writing an informal letter

35 Park Road, Oxford

25th November

Dear Miriam,

1— It was really nice to get your letter and hear from you again. The new house sounds fabulous. I am really sorry that I haven't kept in touch but things at work and home have been really busy lately.

2— As for us, we're all well, and life is pretty much the same as ever. You'll be pleased to hear that Peter finally got his promotion. Both the kids are growing up fast – Marco has taken up the saxophone and Juliet is in another play. One piece of sad news – you'll be sorry to hear that our lovely old cat passed away at Christmas.

3— By the way, you'll never guess who I bumped into the other day. Do you remember Harriet Drake from school? She's been working in Africa for two years. What's more, she has met a widower and they are planning to get married next year. She's lost a lot of weight and looks five years younger.

4— Talking of foreign locations, our other news is that we're taking the kids to Florida in May. I was wondering if you could put us up the night before our early morning flight? It would give us the chance to catch up on all our news.

I must hurry if I am going to catch the post. I'll give you

5— a ring later in the week. Bye for now.

Lots of love   Gemma

1 Read the letter. Complete the notes for paragraphs **1** to **5**.

1 thanks for _____   response to _____
  apologies for _____
2 good news _____   bad news _____
3 surprise news _____
4 future plans _____   asking for a favour _____
5 leave-taking _____   promise to _____

2 Use the paragraph notes. Write an informal letter.

How to open and close letters

Writing	Opening	Ending
to the person you love (Anna)	(My) dear Max,	All my love
to a female friend / family (Anna)	Dear Jane / Mum,	Lots of love
between two male friends	Dear David,	All the best (Jeff)
to a friendly colleague	Dear Janet,	Best wishes / Regards (Anna)
formally	Dear Janet / Ms Wilson,	Yours sincerely (Anna Grey)
	Dear Sir / Madam,	Yours faithfully (Anna Grey)

05

1 Put the conversation in order.

- [1] So where do you come from?
- [ ] So do you miss it? Would you like to go back there to live?
- [ ] Very pleasant. It's changed a lot though; it's not as quiet as it used to be.
- [ ] We used to go for wonderful walks by the river, and to concerts in King's College Chapel.
- [ ] No I haven't, but I'd like to. Is it like Oxford?
- [ ] So what's it like now?
- [ ] I was born and brought up in Cambridge. Have you been there?
- [ ] Nowadays it's much busier, with hi-tech industries like computer firms, attracted by the university, and unfortunately, a lot of tourism. It feels crowded all the time.
- [ ] Wasn't it rather boring? What was there to do?
- [ ] And what was it like growing up in a small town?
- [ ] I don't think so. I like living in London too much.
- [ ] Yes, in the sense that they're both university towns, of course. Cambridge is a bit smaller.

2 ⏱ **Five-minute brainstorm** Write as many positive and negative things about your home town as you can.

3 Reply using short questions.

1 I went to see Cindy last night. *Oh, did you?*
2 I'd never eat in that place again.
3 My parents weren't very pleased with my results.
4 It's Peter's birthday tomorrow.
5 She's always complaining about something.
6 We don't have to leave yet.
7 I'll give you a lift to the station.

06

4 Complete the sentences to express obligation, permission, or necessity.

1 I _wasn't allowed to drink_ wine until I was eighteen. (drink)
2 You are a really silly boy; you _____ me never to do that again. (promise)
3 I _____ a lot of travelling for my job. (do)
4 Passengers _____ in this taxi. (eat or drink)
5 She _____ make up at school, but she does! (wear)
6 Is that the time? I really _____ . (go)

7 I _____ my mother because I spoke to her this morning. (not ring)
8 You _____ and see 'Saving Private Ryan'. It's fantastic. (go)
9 It's free. You _____ . (pay)
10 Passengers _____ their tickets until the end of the journey. (keep)
11 You _____ near the edge of the platform. (stand)
12 He _____ his homework before he could watch TV. (finish)
13 Karen _____ as long as she promised to be home by midnight. (go out)

5 Complete the sentences with *didn't need to* or *needn't have*.

1 I didn't have to go to work yesterday so *I didn't need to get up early*. / **get up early**
2 Why didn't you tell me Julia was coming in her car? ... / **bring mine**
3 **drive home fast** / ... because nobody was in when he arrived anyway.
4 **put on clean clothes** / ... because she wanted to do some gardening.
5 They phoned to tell me my appointment was cancelled so ... / **go into town**
6 They had dinner on the plane so ... / **cook a meal**

07

6 **Test your memory for polite requests** Write the words in the correct order.

1 you could the back possibly keep at quiet! *Could you possibly keep quiet at the back!*
2 I do think weekend borrow could you your drill this?
3 all right is open it I the window if?
4 anyone mind if watch news I does the?
5 you do to if know bank here there's a happen near?
6 could I if check you was these me wondering figures help.
7 wedding be it film possible to the would?

7 Write replies for **1** to **7** above.

1 ... but I'm going to be using it this weekend.
2 ... I'm very cold.
3 ... go ahead.
4 ... I'm a stranger here myself.
5 ... in about ten minutes.
6 ... use video cameras in the church.

08

Complete the text with a word to do with memory.

Professor Greenstock had a fantastic [1]_____ for mathematical formulae having [2]_____ hundreds. His everyday life, however, was disastrous as he was so [3]_____. His office, briefcase, and even his clothes were covered in yellow stickers as [4]_____ of the simplest tasks. There are many [5]_____ tales about the professor. For instance, one day he arrived home after a day out only to receive an angry phone call from his wife; they had stopped at a motorway service station and he had [6]_____ to bring her home. I even [7]_____ having a long conversation with him outside a [8]_____ shop although he didn't have the faintest idea who I was. "Could you [9]_____ me which way I was walking?" he asked when we had finished. "Certainly, Professor," I replied, "You were going that way, past the war [10]_____. "Ah excellent," he replied, "that means I have had my lunch then." And with that he went on his way.

Writing a letter of enquiry

Your reference *GER/25/QT*

25th September

Mrs J. Marshall
'Homestays in England'
14 South Drive
Bournemouth
BN6 32T

Dear Mrs Marshall,

Paragraph 1
Thanks for information, reason for writing

Thank you for the details of my trip to Bournemouth which I have just received. I am delighted that I am going to be staying so near the school. There are a few questions I would like to ask about my accommodation arrangements.

Paragraph 2
List of questions

First of all, I was wondering if it would be possible to bring my car. Will there be parking space where I am staying? Secondly, I am a keen musician and play the trumpet in a jazz band back home. Will anyone mind if I practise regularly? Also, do you happen to know how I can get in touch with local bands, as I would like to continue playing while I am in Britain. Finally, my girlfriend would like to come and visit for a long weekend from time to time; would it be all right for her to stay with me?

Paragraph 3
Apology for any inconvenience, leave-taking

Could you possibly let me know the answers to these queries before I travel on the 8th. You can contact me by phone on 00 49 30 555 3421. I am sorry to bother you but I would rather everything was clear in advance. I am looking forward to my study course in Bournemouth and to improving my English.

Yours sincerely

Michael Jaeger

1 Read the letter. Why is Michael coming to England?

2 Imagine you are coming to England. Write a similar letter using personal information.

How to ask for information

- include a reference number (so the organization can refer easily to previous correspondence)
- open and close appropriately (Dear Mrs ... / Yours sincerely)
- use polite / tentative requests (Would it be possible ...? / Will anyone mind if ...?)
- put your requests in order (First of all, Secondly, Also, Finally)
- say when you need the information by (Could you let me know before ...)
- apologize for any inconvenience (I am sorry to bother you)
- say you are excited about the trip (I am looking forward to ...)

09

1 Complete the sentences with multi-word verbs.

1 In Britain, you have to _give way_ to the traffic on a roundabout.

2 Don't forget to _____ here. I'm sure there are speed cameras.

3 Sorry I'm so late. I _____ petrol on the motorway!

4 That's my house. Can you _____ just after the traffic lights?

5 I'll just _____ here and you can pop into the shop.

6 I've got to go and _____ Malcolm from the airport.

7 I _____ a fox; it just ran into the road.

2 Rewrite with extreme adjectives and modifiers where necessary.

1 I feel **very tired**. I've been shopping all day.
absolutely exhausted

2 This bathroom is **dirty**. What have you been up to?

3 That ride was **frightening**. Never again!

4 She was **very angry** when she saw the phone bill.

5 They live in a **big** villa on the coast.

6 This book is **very interesting**; I can't put it down.

7 The film was **really good**; you should have come with us.

8 His room was so **small** he had to stand on the bed to close the door.

9 He was **very shocked** when the waiter gave him the bill.

10 What's that **horrible** smell? He's not cooking cabbage again, is he?

10

3 ⏰ **Five-minute brainstorm** Write as many sentences about driving as you can. Use vocabulary from the following headings.

OPERATING THE CAR	PARTS OF A CAR

PENALTIES	PROBLEMS	ROADS

4 Complete the text with past narrative forms.

Paul [1] _had always wanted_ (always want) to cross the States by motorbike. When he [2] _____ (save) enough money, he [3] _____ (fly) to San Francisco. He [4] _____ (find) a hotel where the owner [5] _____ (happen) to have a Harley for sale. It [6] _____ (be left) by a guest and [7] _____ (lie) under a sheet for years. Paul [8] _____ (buy) it for $1,000 and [9] _____ (leave) the next day. On the third day he [10] _____ (only ride) for an hour when the bike suddenly [11] _____ (break down). Luckily, he [12] _____ (not wait) long before a man in a pick-up truck [13] _____ (pull over) and took him to a garage. While he [14] _____ (have) a coffee in a diner the garage owner [15] _____ (come) to see him. He said he [16] _____ (collect) Harleys for years but [17] _____ (not have) Paul's model. He [18] _____ (offer) him $3,000 and a new bike in exchange. Paul [19] _____ (can't) believe his luck. However, a look of triumph [20] _____ (flash) across the garage owner's face as he [21] _____ (give) Paul the keys and cash. Later, as Paul [22] _____ (take) his things from under the seat he [23] _____ (notice) a small plate he [24] _____ (not see) before. It [25] _____ (say): 'To my friend James Dean, happy riding, Elvis.'

5 Complete the sentences with *after* or *afterwards*.

1 _____After_____ he had saved enough money he went to the States.

2 He arrived in San Francisco and _____ he found a hotel.

3 Paul paid cash for the bike but _____ a few days, it broke down.

4 Luckily, someone picked him up shortly _____ .

5 Paul noticed the plate _____ he had accepted the money.

11

6 Find an opposite for the words in **bold**.

1 an **attractive** woman	_plain_	an **elaborate** meal
2 a **spicy** curry	_____	a **strong** cigarette
3 **still** water	_____	a **boring** performance
4 a **wet** day	_____	a **sweet** wine
5 a **sour** taste	_____	a **bitter** moment
6 **plain** food	_____	a **poor** man
7 an **alcoholic** drink	_____	a **hard** bed

7 **Test your memory for recommendations** Match **1** to **9** with **a** to **i**.

1 It's an intriguing play

2 What a tedious film!

3 That club's far too trendy.

4 The best thing about it was

5 You really should

6 The menu was limited

7 Turner's stormy seascapes

8 There are some stunning designs

9 Their new album is predictable

a It's really not my sort of place at all.

b and their live concert was mediocre.

c read it for yourself.

d I wouldn't bother going if I were you.

e and the food uninspiring.

f the gripping plot.

g in Conran's spring collection.

h set in America after the Civil War.

i are wonderfully atmospheric.

12

8 Word challenge Find and correct the confused words.

1 I'd like to change this book. The ~~recipe~~ is in the bag.
   receipt

2 Cheating in an exam! Aren't you embarrassed of yourself?

3 If you go to Milan, take the possibility to go to the opera.

4 The sun's very hot. Go and sit in the shadow or you'll burn.

5 Good health is worthless, there's no doubt about it.

6 Our distributor keeps our stock in a department store.

7 When I got stuck in deep snow, I felt as unhelpful as a baby.

8 I have an imagination about living on a tropical island.

9 They have a beautiful villa on the beach of Lake Como.

10 Don't be so middle ages, Howard! Get up and dance.

9 Complete the sentences with an expression with *mind*.

1 Work's very busy at the moment – *I've got a lot on my mind*.

2 You can't come tonight? _____ , some other time.

3 _____ your head when you stand up.

4 Is it all right if I _____ ? I feel quite strongly about this.

5 _____ if Julian stays the night?

6 I really can't _____ . Which one should I choose?

7 Where have you been? Your mother has been _____ with worry.

Writing a narrative

Paragraph 1
Setting the scene for the story

Rebecca Crowther will never forget last Christmas. A log fire blazed and crackled in the fireplace, while outside the snow sparkled on the Yorkshire countryside. All the presents had been wrapped up and placed lovingly under the brightly-decorated Christmas tree. It was going to be a marvellous Christmas.

Paragraph 2
Introducing the main character, setting events in motion

However, the family's dog Reggie, a 45-kilo Labrador with a healthy appetite, was feeling rather neglected. While the family were sitting down to a traditional lunch the dog was wondering what had happened to his. The delicious smells made the normally good-tempered Reggie feel desperately hungry. So while the Crowthers were eating their turkey, Reggie went off to see what he could find. Minutes later, as the family were attacking the pudding, the dog came across a package which interested him.

Paragraph 3
Focus of the story

After their meal they went in search of the presents, the children excitedly leading the way. Rebecca had been especially looking forward to seeing Maurice's face when he opened the mobile phone she had bought him. However, although everyone else's presents were under the tree, poor Maurice's had disappeared. At first Rebecca thought she was going out of her mind. She couldn't think what could have happened to it. She looked all round the house but it was nowhere to be found. Then their daughter, Faith, had a bright idea. 'Why not', she suggested, 'try calling the number of the mobile?'

Paragraph 4
Development of the drama

All of a sudden, the dog started to ring! Nobody was more surprised than Reggie. Yes, as you can guess, not only had he eaten the phone and wrapping paper but he had swallowed it in one single go. They were absolutely horrified, and rushed Reggie off to the vet for a check-up. They were too worried to be angry with him and thought he would have to have an emergency operation.

Paragraph 5
Conclusion

---

1 Read the story. Think of a suitable title.

2 Write the final paragraph.

How to create atmosphere

- Choose vocabulary carefully to create the atmosphere of Christmas
  lovingly, brightly-decorated, sparkle, blaze
- Use the past continuous tense to explain what's going on
  the family were sitting down / the dog was wondering
- Use direct speech to make a narrative more immediate and dramatic
- Use comments directed to the reader to involve them in the story
  Yes, as you can guess …
- Make the final sentence of each paragraph prepare the reader for the development of the story in the next

13

1 Complete the story with multi-word verbs.

This morning I had to contact Mrs Peabody at the tax office. I [1] *looked up* the number in the phone book but it wasn't listed so I [2] _____ Directory Enquiries who eventually gave me the number. When someone finally [3] _____ the phone they tried to [4] _____ to her extension, but the line went dead and I realized I had been [5] _____. Then I couldn't [6] _____ because her line was engaged. The third time I called I had to [7] _____ for more than five minutes while they looked for her. When they found her I could hardly hear her and had to ask her to [8] _____. And after all that, she was so rude and unhelpful that I simply [9] _____.

2 **Test your memory for phoning** Order the conversation.

☐ Hello, <u>I'm afraid</u> she's in a meeting, but if you'd like to give me your number I'll make sure she <u>returns your call</u>.

☐ My name's Lisa Farrow, I came for an interview last week.

☐ I need to know urgently whether I'm going to be called for a second interview.

☐ And can I ask what it is in connection with?

[1] Good morning, <u>could I speak to</u> Mrs King, please?

☐ That's very kind of you.

☐ All right, Ms Farrow, could you <u>hold the line</u>? I'll see if Mrs King's available.

☐ <u>May I ask who's calling</u>, please?

☐ <u>Certainly</u>.

3 Write less formal equivalents of the underlined phrases in ex. 2.

14

4 Complete the sentences with an appropriate future form.

1 We _____ (buy) a new car next year.

2 Can't you get it to work? I _____ (show) you.

3 I _____ (wait) for you in arrivals when you land.

4 Your train _____ (leave) Waterloo at 13.45.

5 Look at those clouds! I'm sure _____ (rain).

6 This time tomorrow we _____ (lie) on a beach.

7 Sorry, I can't. I _____ (go out) tonight.

8 They _____ (stay) with Sally on Friday.

9 You must buy one; you _____ (not regret) it.

10 We _____ (finish) the job by the weekend.

5 Complete the text with a form of the future perfect, the future continuous, or *will*.

Ever thought what football will be like in the future?

Experts have put their heads together and come up with a few predictions for the year 2020. By then they [1] _____ (close) most of the stadiums because not enough people [2] _____ (go) to matches. Sadly, a lot of small clubs [3] _____ (disappear) and there [4] _____ (be) a European super league. In fact, for important matches they [5] _____ (pay) people to go along and watch just to create some atmosphere. Arguments about whether the ball has crossed the goal line [6] _____ (become) a thing of the past. It's highly likely that there [7] _____ (be) beams across the goal posts and the players themselves [8] _____ (wear) electronic tags for years. This means the referee [9] _____ (be automatically informed) if anyone is off-side. Matches [10] _____ (play) on artificial grass and the player of the match elected on the Internet by viewers.

6 Rephrase the words in **bold** using adjectival phrases.

1 They are **certain to be** late, they always are.

2 According to the timetable the train **should** arrive now.

3 **There's a strong possibility** that they'll offer her the job.

4 I **really don't think** she'll get that promotion.

5 We're **expecting Mr Ross** to contact us next week.

6 I'm **sure that coat** will have been sold. It was a bargain!

15

7 **Word challenge** Complete the adjectives describing image. Check on *p.44*.

1 D Y _ _ _ _ _ _
2 S M _ _ _
3 A S _ _ _ _ _ _
4 F A _ _ _
5 C O _ _ _ _ _ _ _
6 O V _ _ - _ _ _ _ _
7 E L _ _ _
8 A D _ _ _ _ _ _

8 Rephrase the words in **bold** using an expression with *look*.

1 Could you **take care of** my dogs while I'm away?

2 **Find out what** this word **means** in your dictionary.

3 Mathilde **can't wait to start** her new job.

4 I **admire** Tony because he's taught me so much.

5 I'm **trying to find** a new jacket in the sales.

6 Well, it **seemed to be** a good job from the advert.

7 Since she was promoted Janet **doesn't think** her old colleagues **are good enough for her**.

8 There's something wrong here; let's **find out more about** it.

16

9 ⏱ **Five-minute brainstorm** Write as many words and expressions under the headings as you can.

APPLYING FOR A JOB	LOSING / NOT HAVING A JOB

ADJECTIVES TO DESCRIBE JOBS

10 **Quick crossword** Complete the puzzle by following the clues **1** to **12**. Find the mystery word.

Clues

1 What workers are made when their factory closes.
2 Employers usually ask job applicants for these.
3 What you will be given if you don't do your job well! (two words)
4 You will be ... (**3** more formally)
5 The form job-hunters fill in.
6 What you get if you study hard at school / college / university.
7 What you go on if you receive unemployment benefit from the government.
8 Monthly wages.
9 Extra hours for extra money.
10 The kind of job that makes you anxious and worried all the time (adjective).
11 The kind of job that stretches and stimulates you (adjective).
12 What you might go on if you're not happy with your working conditions.

```
1
2
3
4
5
6
7
8
9
10
11
12
```

Writing a job application letter

Ref: AS674
Mrs A. Crufts
Walkies!
15 Washington St.
Brighton BN6 7BA

Dear Mrs Crufts,

I am writing to apply for the job of animal carer which I saw advertised in the Evening Standard on Friday 27th.

I am 20 years old and come from near Florence in Italy. I have taken a year off my studies to improve my English. I am looking for a part-time job which doesn't involve working afternoons, as I attend English classes from 1.30 to 5.00 p.m.

I have a lot of experience of looking after all kinds of animals, not only because I was brought up on a farm, but also because I am training to be a vet, so ·I am well-qualified to attend to the animals' health and well-being. I am very fit (I am a keen runner and swimmer) and I am used to getting up early. My language skills (I speak Italian and French) may be useful if you deal with foreign clients.

I enclose my CV and references for your information. If you still have vacancies for this job I would be interested in receiving further information regarding hours and rates of pay.

I look forward to hearing from you.

Yours sincerely

Mathilde Rossi

Mathilde Rossi (Miss)

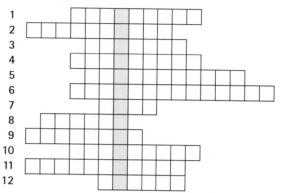

WANTED Animal carers for morning and evening pet-sitting / dog-walking while owners are away. Good rates of pay. Write to Mrs Annabel Crufts at *Walkies!* Ref: AS674

1 Read the application letter. Order the headings.

- closing where you know the person's name ☐
- opening where you know the person's name [1]
- says where she saw the advertisement ☐
- mentions enclosures ☐
- request for further information ☐
- reason for writing ☐
- details of skills and experience ☐
- why she wants the job ☐

2 Write an application for a part-time job in a bar.

How to apply for a job

- Make your covering letter short and clear
- Open and close the letter appropriately
- Give a few relevant and interesting details about yourself
- Say why you want the job and why you're suitable
- Enclose further information, e.g. CV, references
- If you're not sure, get someone to check your English
- Keep a copy of the advert and the letter

17

1 Word challenge Make complete words.

1	PILG*rimage*	HURE
2	DEPA	AGE
3	FOL	HPLACE
4	BROC	RTURE
5	SIGH	~~RIMAGE~~
6	HERIT	KLORE
7	BIRT	MORATE
8	EXCU	IGHT
9	COMME	TSEE
10	OVERN	RSION

2 Match the definitions to **1** to **10** above.

a Opposite of arrival. ☐

b Spending the night. ☐

c A journey to a place of religious importance. ☐ 1

d A trip to a place of interest, often by coach. ☐

e What people like to do in historic cities. ☐

f Where someone important was born. ☐

g A magazine with details of holidays and prices. ☐

h The songs, dances and traditions of ordinary people. ☐

i Cultural sites and places of beauty are part of this. ☐

j To honour the memory of a person or event. ☐

3 Underline the correct form.

Lucy   What do you feel like ¹**to do/doing** this summer?

Damien I'm not sure, but I ²**fancy/'d like** going somewhere different.

Lucy   Tell you what; why don't we ³**to drive/drive** to the mountains?

Damien I 'd rather ⁴**go/going** to the sea myself.

Lucy   Oh yes, you're not that keen ⁵**on/for** heights, are you?

Damien How about ⁶**to have/having** a cycling holiday in France? We could always ⁷**stay/staying** in hotels if it rains.

Lucy   I suppose so, although we'd better ⁸**check/to check** with the twins first.

Damien You're right. Let's ⁹**see/seeing** what they say. They might prefer ¹⁰**to do/doing** their own thing.

Lucy   I understand what you ¹¹**'re saying/say**, but aren't they a bit young ¹²**to have/having** a holiday on their own. They're only sixteen.

18

4 Write similar sentences.

1 Nobody swam faster than Jo.

  Jo was *the fastest swimmer*   .

2 Paul is the rudest man I know.

  Nobody I know is _____ .

3 The Lodge Hotel doesn't have nearly as many facilities as the Park Hotel.

  The Lodge Hotel has far _____ .

4 I think Paris is much more elegant than London.

  London is a lot _____

5 Is this the best hotel in this town?

  Isn't there _____ .

6 He isn't quite as ill as yesterday.

  He feels slightly _____

7 I've never eaten such an awful meal.

  This is _____ .

8 As last night continued it became progressively colder.

  It got _____ .

9 Cathy is a much faster driver than Peter.

  Peter _____ .

10 Jason is a bad cook but Simon is terrible.

  Simon is an even _____ .

19

5 Test your memory for indirect questions Avoid answering the questions in six different ways.

1 Have you ever stolen anything?
  I'd like you to tell me whether you've ever stolen anything.
  Mind your own business.

2 How much did you earn last year?

3 How long have you been driving?

4 Do you have any health problems?

5 Do you believe in life after death?

6 How old are you?

7 How do you get on with your parents?

20

6 ☼ **Five-minute brainstorm** Write adjectives.

SOMEONE WHO

1 doesn't trust other people   *suspicious*

2 is ruled by affairs of the heart   _____

3 is shy and hides their feelings   _____

4 thinks they are superior to others   _____

5 you can really depend on   _____

6 isn't willing to accept new ideas   _____

SOMEWHERE WHICH

7 is out of touch with the life of the capital   _____

8 is comfortable with a mix of cultures and attitudes   _____

9 makes outsiders feel accepted   _____

10 has highly developed manners and customs   _____

7 Mark the stress. Write an example for each adjective.

1 <u>sen</u>sitive O-o-o *My brother is very sensitive to criticism.*

2 lively   5 easy-going   8 forward-thinking

3 modest   6 tolerant   9 down-to-earth

4 polite   7 individualist   10 genuine

Writing a letter of complaint

The Manager
The Grand Hotel
York Rd
Harrogate
HG4 9SP

Dear Sir/Madam,

Paragraph 1
Background to the complaint

My husband and I have just returned from a weekend at your hotel. We had been looking forward to a peaceful break in luxurious surroundings, as promised in your brochure, and recommended by friends. Unfortunately, the weekend did not live up to our expectations.

Paragraph 2
Main complaint / details

Our main complaint is that, despite having booked several months in advance, when we arrived we were told that the main hotel was full with conference delegates and we were put in an annex behind the hotel. To begin with, the room we were given was extremely cold. The noise of traffic kept us awake most of the night because the annex is right beside the main road. In addition, the bed was uncomfortable because the mattress was old and lumpy. Finally, to add insult to injury, the bathroom had not been cleaned.

Paragraph 3
Level of disappointment

Clearly the accommodation in this part of the hotel is not up to the high standard of the main building. We had paid in advance, however, we would not have proceeded with the booking if we had known that a room in the main hotel would not be available. We are particularly disappointed since the weekend was a special occasion for us, to celebrate my husband's birthday. We are extremely annoyed that, apparently, large parties take priority over individual guests regardless of when bookings are received.

Paragraph 4
Request for compensation

Despite our dissatisfaction with the room, we have no complaint with the lovely food, or high standard of service from the staff. We are sure that you would wish us and our friends to use the hotel again. We trust therefore that you will take this matter seriously, and look forward to hearing from you by return with an appropriate offer of compensation.

Yours faithfully

Mrs. M. S. Bayes

1 Read the letter. What kind of problems were there?
2 Write a letter of complaint about a product or service you are dissatisfied with.

How to complain effectively

Be firm

• Use formal language: we would not have proceeded (= not gone ahead with), we trust that ... (we are sure that ...)
• Give specific examples: the main hotel was full, the room was cold
• Order your points logically: to begin with, in addition, finally
• Make your point strongly: extremely cold, particularly disappointed
• Don't be aggressive. Use passive forms to suggest group rather than personal blame: we were told, we were put
• Suggest a time-limit for a reply: by return
• Indicate that you expect a positive response: we trust that ..., we look forward to ...

Elicit sympathy

• Explain the background: we had been looking forward to a peaceful break, the weekend was a special occasion
• Be persuasive: unfortunately, despite, therefore

Show good faith

• Mention the good things: lovely food, high standard of service
• Indicate that you could be persuaded to forgive: we are sure that you would wish us to return

21

1 Complete the text with signals and repetition.

> [1]_____, shall we start? Here's the report on the Film Festival for the last three years. Sadly, [2]_____ people are coming each year. [3]_____, there's a big fair on the same night. Apparently, it was terribly crowded this year; [4]_____ of people went there. [5]_____, I have heard that other Festivals are having similar problems. [6]_____, next year we'll be choosing a different weekend, and including children's films, so that, hopefully, [7]_____ families will be attracted.

2 ⏱ **Five-minute brainstorm** Replace the words in **bold** with an expression with *take*.

1 The film **is set** in the reign of King George I. *takes place*
2 Could you **look after** my cat this weekend?
3 You'll only succeed if you really **care about** your work.
4 Over 200,000 people **participated** in the demonstration.
5 He **exploited** confidential information to buy cheap shares.
6 He just **presumed** that he could stay for as long as he wanted.
7 She doesn't **enjoy doing** anything.

22

3 Read the text and write passive sentences.

> **ALEXANDER FLEMING** discovered penicillin quite by accident. It saved the lives of hundreds of thousands of soldiers in World War II and doctors have used penicillin to fight infection ever since. Nowadays chemists can mass-produce antibiotics in laboratories. However, the effects are not all positive. Vets give huge quantities of antibiotics to farm animals and this is seriously affecting the human immune system. Also, because antibiotics force the bacteria they attack to mutate, scientists are having to invent stronger and stronger versions. Today's typical dose of antibiotics would have killed patients 50 years ago. Such predictions might have shocked Sir Alexander Fleming.

1 Penicillin _____ .
2 The lives _____ .
3 Antibiotics _____ .
4 Farm animals _____ .
5 The human immune system _____ .
6 Stronger versions _____ .
7 Patients 50 years ago _____ .
8 Sir Alexander Fleming _____ .

4 Complete with passive forms where appropriate.

The very last thing in beauty treatment

It was the ambition of all Ancient Egyptians to [1] *be mummified* (mummify) when they [2]_____ (die). However, this process [3]_____ (can / only / afford) the very wealthy and the Pharoahs. First of all, the brains [4]_____ (remove) by embalmers. They [5]_____ (pull out) through the nose with a special hook. The internal organs, except for the heart, [6]_____ (store) in special jars. The body [7]_____ (wash) in palm wine and [8]_____ (preserve) by packing it in a kind of sodium carbonate called natron. After a hundred days the body [9]_____ (fill up) with cloth and mud, and the skin [10]_____ (oil and wax). Next, several kilometres of oily bandages [11]_____ (wrap) around the mummy before it [12]_____ (put) in its coffin with gold and jewels. Magic charms [13]_____ (place) between the layers of bandages so that when the Pharoah [14]_____ (arrive) in the Underworld, his heart wouldn't [15]_____ (weigh) more than a feather. According to the Ancient Egyptians, heavy hearts [16]_____ (eat up) by a monster waiting by the scales. Sadly, by the end of the 19th century, many of the mummies and treasures [17]_____ (disappear), stolen by thieves and archaeologists. ○

5 Complete the sentences using *have* or *get* and the correct form of the words in brackets.

1 I must (my jacket / clean). It's filthy.
2 We need to (car / service) before we go away.
3 My mother has finally decided to (central heating / put in).
4 I'm going to (ring / value) for the insurance company.
5 When did you (hair / cut)? It looks nice.

23

6 Complete the sentences with *be / get used to* + *-ing* form or *used to* + base form. Choose a suitable verb.

1 I just can't *get used to living* abroad.
2 It's hard to believe that George _____ the good-looking young man in that photo.
3 At first I found driving on the left really difficult. I _____ nightmares about roundabouts. Now, I'm a bit more _____ on the wrong side of the road.

4 When he lived at home his mother _____ everything. Now he lives alone he simply isn't _____ after himself.

5 When her brother was born Melissa was extremely jealous because she was so _____ the centre of attention.

6 Marilyn found it hard to _____ on the dole after losing her job.

7 I know you, didn't you _____ yoga classes?

8 Do you think you'll ever _____ English food?

9 I'm not _____ my married name!

10 She's so outgoing – you wouldn't think she _____ shy.

7 Test your memory for giving a tour You are a castle guide. How do you ... ?

1 welcome visitors to the castle
2 introduce yourself as the guide, and explain what you're going to do
3 check that people are present
4 ask people to look carefully at the 15th century tapestries
5 indicate a new stage of the tour / talk
6 ask people to come with you to visit the dungeon
7 warn people about the steep stairs

8 Write words which connect the phrases either side.

1	dig for gold	_mine_	belonging to me
2	like a small rat	_____	a computer control
3	e.g. Mother Theresa	_____	a computer symbol
4	the noise when you turn on the light	_____	the noise made by 1 above
5	pull something heavy	_____	move something on a screen
6	read quickly	_____	trace electronically
7	small sharp object	_____	number for withdrawing money
8	something to look through	_____	information square on a screen

9 Word challenge
Find twelve technology words, going from top to bottom and left to right. Check on *p.68*.

```
P R I N T E R A D A M S
A F H E P C R O U B A B
S E N B K E Y B O A R D
S C U Y A B E U F R A T
W I T H D R A W S C O C
O D W A I A F B G O N A
R E Y R B A C K U P L S
D S C C K E U E N E I H
E L D S E A R C H I N C
D E L K T H S O M A E A
F N G T T N O P J S M R
L S A V E R R E W I N D
```

Writing instructions

Bath time

In Japan we shower first to clean our bodies and then relax in a deliciously hot bath of clean water. Possibly because of water shortages, the British have a bath or a shower – it is absolutely forbidden to do both.

Instructions

1 Fill bath no more than ten cms (remember, water is precious).

2 Place small yellow plastic duck on surface of water.

3 Sit upright in water and wash your body with soap. To wash your hair, kneel and put hair in water.

4 Lie back and soak your body in dirty water (no more than 15 mins).

5 Get out of bath and then rub dirty water off your body with clean towel until you feel hot and towel is dirty.

6 Clean and dry duck. (If duck is clean, you are clean.)

'My Nightmare in England' by Colin Lynes and Kotaro Sarai, p11

1 Read the instructions. How do you know the writer is being funny?

2 Write instructions for an unusual dance, recipe, or activity from your country.

How to make instructions clear

• Use the imperative or the impersonal *you*: *Fill bath* or *You fill the bath*. With the imperative you can leave out articles to make the instructions very simple

• Put the instructions in order. Use a numbered list or connectors: *First of all / To begin with, Next / After that / Afterwards / When you've done ..., Lastly / Finally*

• Be brief, use abbreviations (cms / mins)

• Include reminders: *Remember / Don't forget to ... / no more than ...*, and warnings: *Be careful not to ... / Mind you don't ...*

• Add notes (in brackets) to make things clear

25

1 ⏱ **Five minute brainstorm** Replace the words in **bold** with an expression with *thing*.

1 It's fine to travel cheaply, but **very risky** to hitchhike. *quite another thing*

2 **Having examined all the evidence**, I think she must be guilty.

3 He loves bunjee-jumping and all that **sort of stuff**.

4 They won the match, that's **all that's important**.

5 Just because it's **fashionable** doesn't mean that you have to copy everyone else.

6 Shall we go with them or shall we **do as we please**?

7 OK, they're in love, but the **point is** she's fifteen years older than him.

2 Rewrite the sentences using the KEY word.

1 I think we should ban smoking in public places. OPINION
In my opinion smoking should be banned in public places.

2 Mrs Green says it's wrong to eat meat. ACCORDING

3 I think hanging is too kind for some criminals. CONCERNED

4 I really don't think the government should sell arms to poor countries. BE ALLOWED

5 Child labour in factories is just slavery by a different name. LIKE

6 That idea is really stupid. WHAT

7 I'm not sure that it's such a good idea. PERSONALLY

8 It's pointless trying to make him understand. WASTE

26

3 Complete the dialogue. Use a modal verb and an appropriate form of the verbs below.

come	be (x2)	break	take	hang
stand	wait	blow in	get in	

Watson   Look Holmes, the murderer ¹ *must have come* through this window and hanged Sir Rodney.

Holmes   No Watson, he or she ² _____ from outside. Observe, the broken glass is outside, so the window ³ _____ from the inside.

Watson   But the door was locked and there were no keys. Someone ⁴ _____ them, I suppose, or else ...

Holmes   Yes, it ⁵ _____ someone he knew. Who are our suspects?

Watson   Well, Grimes the butler, Melissa, his daughter, or the housekeeper, Mrs Harkness. It ⁶ _____ any of the three.

Holmes   But there is one other suspect, Sir Rodney himself.

Watson   He ⁷ _____ himself. There was nothing for him to stand on.

Holmes   But what does the water on the floor tell you?

Watson   Well, the rain ⁸ _____ through the broken window.

Holmes   No, he ⁹ _____ on a block of ice and waited for it to melt.

Watson   How awful! He ¹⁰ _____ for hours. You're a genius, Holmes!

27

4 Correct the sentences.

1 It was a wonderful opportunity but she turned down it.

2 We've got our old jobs to fall back if things go wrong.

3 I'm really looking forward to start the new term.

4 The play was carried on even though the main actor was ill.

5 She gave up to smoke when she became pregnant.

6 I took part the London marathon last year.

5 **Test your memory for criticizing and blaming** Write similar sentences.

1 Why didn't you take the job to help your family?
You should *have taken the job* _____ .

2 You wasted an opportunity to make a fortune.
You could _____ .

3 He said it was my fault that we lost the match.
He blamed _____ .

4 I really don't understand why he did such a terrible thing.
Why _____ ?

5 I hold you responsible for getting us into this mess.
It's your _____ .

6 You didn't go to your brother's wedding? That's terrible.
You ought _____ .

28

6 **Word challenge** Think of as many words as you can to do with world problems under the headings.

DISASTERS	POLITICS	SPORT
BUSINESS	THE ECONOMY	WAR

7 Find headline synonyms to replace the words in **bold**.

1 The worst thing is that hundreds of **ordinary people** have died. *civilians*

2 Serious **arguments** between ministers have **divided** the government.

3 A charity has given farming **tools** to the **people who suffered in the flood**.

4 The United Nations has **encouraged** both sides to hand over their **guns**.

5 The villagers have been **running away** across the border **trying to find** a safe hiding place.

6 The union representative has threatened to **leave** if the members refuse to **support** him.

7 After the **explosion** the **injured people** were taken to hospital.

8 The Minister of Finance has been **dismissed** for taking bribes.

8 Make nouns from the adjectives below. Complete the sentences.

cruel	~~miserable~~	afraid	poor
homeless	corrupt	unemployed	

1 Seeing refugees living in _misery_ is very distressing.

2 If there's one thing I can't stand it's _____ to animals.

3 Rising _____ will affect millions of people.

4 A parent's greatest _____ is the loss of a child.

5 The _____ of politicians no longer surprises me.

6 They lived in extreme _____ , with little food and limited shelter.

7 As more people move to the city, _____ becomes an increasing problem.

Writing 'for' and 'against'

'Public people don't deserve a private life.' Discuss.

Nowadays, it's hard to find a popular newspaper or magazine which doesn't gossip about the private lives of people in the public eye; the rich and the famous. For the purposes of this essay let us compare two categories of public people; celebrities from the world of sport and entertainment, and public servants. How fair is it that their lives should be put under the microscope?

Let's take celebrities such as film stars. In their early careers they will do almost anything to be noticed. Yet once they are successful they hide behind dark glasses and security guards. In a sense, their lack of privacy is the price they pay for their fame and fortune. It is hard, therefore, to be sympathetic when they complain about media attention. They have chosen a career which puts them on view, and I believe the public have a right to know. Having said that, children are often the innocent victims of their parents' lifestyle. Despite benefiting from wealth and position, cruel and exaggerated media reports must cause them sadness.

Politicians, on the other hand, are in principle in the public eye to do a job. Similarly, a Royal Family is there to play a valued role. It is perhaps true that the way they behave in private tells us about their inner integrity. Personally, I believe their private lives should be respected as long as they carry out their jobs well. Take Clinton for example; does it really matter if the President is a bad husband? Nevertheless, it is important to recognize abuse of public trust, for instance, a government minister who uses his position to obtain personal favours deserves to be exposed, and the media plays a useful role in maintaining the integrity of public servants. All too often, however, too much attention can be tragic. We only have to think of Princess Diana, who would not have been speeding through Paris if she was not being harassed by journalists and photographers.

In conclusion, although freedom of the media is important, it should not be abused. The editors who demand stories and pictures need to learn the difference between what is interesting to the public and what is in the public interest.

---

1 Read the composition. Make the notes for each paragraph.

2 Write a composition with the title 'School shouldn't be compulsory'.

How to plan a composition

- Collect and note down ideas. Read around the topic, e.g. in newspapers. Ask other people what they think
- Prepare a plan. Decide on a introduction, and a conclusion. Argue a different angle in each paragraph
- Define terms from the title, i.e. what you mean by 'public people'.
- Include examples that other people can relate to (*Princess Diana, Take Clinton, for example*)
- Include your own views (*Personally, I believe …*)
- Use questions which you then answer (*Does it really matter if …?*)
- Balance and contrast your arguments (*on the one hand … on the other, nevertheless, yet*)
- Mark your conclusion: *In conclusion, to sum up …* and try to end with a memorable line (*interesting to the public / in the public interest*)

29

1 Test your memory for gossiping Write the words in the correct order.

1 who you'll never guess saw I.   ☐ P
You'll never guess who I saw.

2 breathe won't a word I.   ☐

3 I it well don't believe.   ☐

4 you anyone won't tell promise.   ☐

5 sealed my are lips.   ☐

6 in is the confidence this strictest.   ☐

7 go ears on am I all.   ☐

8 something I heard that might you interest.   ☐

2 Mark the above sentences L for listening to gossip or P for passing on gossip.

30

3 Complete the sentences using the verb in brackets.

1 If she doesn't arrive by six, we (leave).

2 I would have told you if he (give) the book to me.

3 They won't let you in if you (not wear) smart clothes.

4 If only I had listened to her my life (be) different now.

5 He would look a lot better if he (lose) weight.

6 If it hadn't rained this morning, I (play) tennis.

7 I wish I (speak) German as well as Julia.

8 If you had known my father you (get on well) with him.

9 I really wish he (whistle) that stupid tune all the time.

10 If you press this button, someone (come) and help you.

4 Write sentences with a similar meaning.

1 I regret not listening to my mother when I was younger.
I wish I had listened to my mother when I was younger.

2 I don't have a car but I'd like one.
I wish _____ .

3 She didn't pass because she hadn't studied her notes.
If she _____ .

4 I hate it when he smokes in the bedroom.
I wish _____ .

5 I didn't go to the party last night because I felt really tired.
If I _____ .

6 They have a lovely house in the country. I'm so jealous!
I wish I _____ .

7 Your bike was stolen because the lock wasn't secure.
If the lock _____ .

8 It was stupid of me to give him my phone number.
I wish _____ .

5 Read the text. Expand and complete the sentences.

The *Titanic* was on her maiden voyage across the Atlantic from Southampton to New York. It had many rich people on board. Everybody believed it was unsinkable, which explains why there weren't enough lifeboats. The captain ignored iceberg warnings and continued at full speed. Even though it was foggy the *Titanic* was travelling fast, at 22 knots. With no radar they had to rely on lookouts. When a lookout saw the iceberg it was too late to change direction and the ship was going so fast that it was fatally damaged. The first lifeboat contained only eleven people including three millionaires and a director of the *White Star* line. Most of the passengers who died were travelling third class. A passing ship, the *SS California*, didn't stop. Nobody had seen the flares or heard the radio signals. Luckily, the arrival of the *Carpathia* just before the *Titanic* went down meant the total of 1,513 deaths was not higher.

1 If they/not believe/the ship was unsinkable ...

2 If the captain/listen to iceberg warnings ...

3 If it/not be so foggy ...

4 If the ship/not continue at full speed ...

5 If they/have radar ...

6 If the first lifeboats/contain more people ...

7 If the SS *California*/see the flares ...

8 If the *Carpathia*/not be so near ...

31

6 Mark the stress. Write an example for each adjective.

1 ad**ven**turous o-O-o-o
Columbus was the most adventurous sailor of his time.

2	tolerant	8	energetic
3	attractive	9	committed
4	thick-skinned	10	romantic
5	sporty	12	messy
6	chatty	12	demanding
7	passionate	13	patient

7 Write responses using the expressions in the box.

I'd really like your opinion ...	By the way ...
I was wondering if ...	~~Oh dear~~ ...
I hear what you're saying ...	So you're saying ...

1 Your brother scratched Dad's car last night.
Oh dear, I expect he was really angry!

2 Ask someone what they think of your new design.

3 Your employees complain that they want a pay rise.

4 Ask nicely if your boss has time to talk to you now.

5 Acknowledge that you've listened to your assistant complaining about the photocopier breaking down again.

6 Add a question at the end of a conversation.

32

8 ⏱ Five-minute brainstorm Complete the blanks with verbs or particles.

TAKE	_____	a loan
	_____	a company (assume control)
	_____	a commitment
	_____	(start to fly)
_____	ON	= proceed
_____		= survive on
_____		= continue
_____	UP	= raise / educate
_____		= establish
_____		= stop doing
_____	UP WITH	= tolerate
		= have an idea

9 Word challenge Complete the words and match them to the definitions. Check on *p.90*.

1 A real chance   H _ _ _ – _ _ _ R
2 Young, highly skilled person   F _ _ _ _ _ L
   Y _ _ _ E _
3 The idea for a new product   S _ _ – _ _ _ _ F
   I _ _ _ _ _ N
4 To do with money   W _ _ _ – _ D
5 Faith in one's own abilities   O _ _ _ _ M _
   O _ _ _ _ _ _ Y
6 A successful, young, urban professional   A _ _ _ _ N
   E _ _ _ _ _ _ _ _ R
7 Confidence in the future
8 An ambitious and successful person
9 The creator of new businesses
10 The desire that drives us to succeed

Writing a report

FAO   Rupert Beazor, Marketing Director, *Frost's Jams*.
From   Jude Rosen, *Aspire Marketing Consultants*.

Initial Report on *Frost's Connoisseur* range.

_____

The *Connoisseur* range of preserves was launched in November of this year and consisted of four products: *Wild Strawberry, Mountain Raspberry, Vicarage Quince Jelly,* and *Andalucian Marmalade*.

It was well promoted through point-of-sale displays and free samples in supermarkets and an award-winning TV commercial starring Miriam Liebermann, the well-known comedian. Sadly, despite *Frost's* best efforts, sales have been disappointing. *Aspire Marketing* was appointed to carry out consumer research to discover why the range had been unsuccessful. In all, three hundred customers and potential customers were interviewed.

_____

Our research identified four key reasons why the *Connoisseur* range has been unsuccessful.

1 The range was too up-market for *Frost's* regular customers. They felt the price outweighed any benefit associated with an organically produced jam.
2 The jams were perceived as luxury products not for everyday consumption.
3 Potential customers were deterred from buying the jams because they did not associate the brand name with up-market luxury products. Even though they agreed the quality was comparable they preferred to buy luxury jams with well-established brand names.
4 Luxury jams are generally bought as gifts. Purchasers are unlikely to buy such gifts from ordinary supermarkets. Some people felt that the packaging was cheap-looking.

_____

We have identified three possible courses of action.

• to cease production and simply withdraw from this sector of the market.
• to re-launch and re-position the product with improved packaging and remove any reference to *Frost's* from the labels. This would also involve seeking distribution and retail outlets in speciality shops and luxury grocery stores.
• to acquire an existing company with an established reputation as a manufacturer of top quality, luxury jams. We have identified one such company which merits further investigation.

_____

This research shows how powerful *Frost's* image for good quality middle-of-the-range products is. A luxury range would, first of all, have had to distance itself from this image. If the *Connoisseur* range had been launched as an entirely different brand they would probably have had more success. *Frost's* image of good quality everyday products providing value for money has proved to be unsuitable for a luxury product range. In conclusion, we feel that *Frost's* should seriously consider the third option, i.e. the acquisition of a well-known brand in the luxury sector.

1 Read the report and decide where these headings should go.

| *Conclusions* | *Background* | *Recommendations* | *Findings* |

2 Write a similar report for the results of another investigation, e.g.

• an accident at a factory
• complaints to a travel company about one of its hotels
• the fall in students at a language school

How to write a report
• use numbers to list points in order of importance
• use bullets for a list of points of equal importance
• use sub-headings to break the report up into easy-to-read sections

EXTRA ACTIVITIES

02 PERSONAL PROFILES

Speak out   Student A

Read the text and complete the chart on *p.9*. Exchange information with **B**.

> If Tom Payne feels like going to the cinema, all he has to do is step into his living room. 'I have been fascinated by cinemas since I was a child,' explains sixty-three-year-old Tom, who used to be a projectionist at the Astoria cinema in Bournemouth. His 'minima' holds an audience of ten and took him eight years to complete; it features a 1940's projector, red velvet curtains, and a traditional 'Exit' sign. Tom plans to hold two screenings a month for family and friends and even has his sister, Cynthia Miller, to serve ice-creams in the interval.

06 HAPPY TOGETHER

Speak out   Student A

Read the text and make notes under the headings on *p.20*.

Sun City

Sun City West in Arizona is exclusively for the over 55s. Young people aren't allowed to live there so there are no schools or child care. 32,000 people live there. It is a bit like a huge leisure park and there is plenty to do. You can be a volunteer policeman, take up roller-skating or even be a pom-pom girl. There are hundreds of different clubs you can join and courses you can take. You can buy a completely equipped house for around $200,000. You're not allowed to make any noise after 8 pm. Private lawns have to be cut once a week and cars kept in a closed garage. The speed limit is 45 kph. There are around fifteen other towns like Sun City spread throughout the States and the concept is becoming more and more popular.

09 IT HAPPENED TO ME

Speak for yourself

Check the colour choices for each personality type according to Conrad King.

Personality type	Colour choice
1 success-driven, ambitious	black
2 outgoing, spontaneous, creative, easily bored	red
3 stylish, a little self-important	silver
4 cold, distant, logical	white
5 safe, cautious	grey
6 a team player, sociable, unimaginative	blue
7 class- and status-conscious	green
8 depressive	pastel colours

13 GETTING THROUGH

Speak for yourself   Student A

Ask **B** for the telephone numbers of:

The White House   _____
Buckingham Palace   _____
The Hard Rock Cafe   _____

Tell **B** the numbers of:

The Vatican	39 06 359 4568
Sydney Opera House	61 2 442 8523
The Kremlin	70 95 661 231

Speak out   Student A

Situation 1

You saw an advertisement in a local newspaper advertising Labrador puppies for sale. Here are some notes you have made to remind yourself of questions. Ask **B**:

- the puppies' age	- their colour
- if a yellow male is available	- the price
- whether they are vaccinated	- the pedigree
- when it is possible to visit	

Situation 2

You run a hotel with your husband / wife. Your friend, who is a travel agent, is on the phone asking about a booking. You are pleased to hear from him / her. Ask a couple of questions about his / her family and business. You don't know anything about the bookings because you are in charge of the restaurant and your husband / wife deals with the bookings. You can't really help and your husband / wife is busy on the other line. Offer to take a message and make sure that you have your friend's number so that your husband / wife can call back.

15 DRESS FOR SUCCESS

Speak out

You are the interviewers. Decide which of the 'tricky situations' you will test your interviewees with.

Tricky situations

1 — Two people who have to share a room do not get on with each other. What would you do?

2 — Someone on the tour clearly knows more about the history and culture of your country than you do. How can you stop the person from becoming bored or unco-operative?

3 — One of your group has been arrested for shoplifting but insists it was all a mistake. How would you try and settle matters with the shop or the police?

4 — One of your group keeps arriving late back at the bus. The other group members are very fed up with this. What would you do?

5 — A young group member is clearly very home-sick and cries for his / her parents. How would you help them?

16 CATS AND RATS

Vocabulary   Group A

Check your definitions from *p.47*. Test a partner from Group **B**.

application form	special form you fill in to apply for a job
references	letter or statement describing someone's ability or character
qualifications	exams you have passed or courses you have completed
part-time	for only some hours of the working week (usually about 20)
skills	abilities which are required to do a job well

20 WHO DO YOU THINK YOU ARE?

Speak for yourself

Check the survey results from *p.57*.

Survey results

1	Sweden	3	Italy	5	Greece	7	Britain
2	France	4	Denmark	6	Germany	8	Britain

Vocabulary

Mark what opinions you think foreigners have of you. Join the different points for a profile of your national character, e.g. *modest* ——×—— *arrogant*

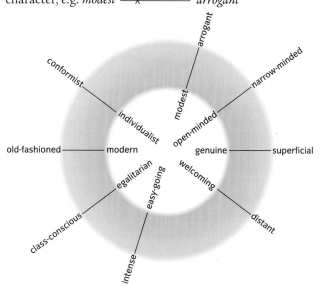

25 INSTANT OPINIONS

Speak for yourself

Use these facts to help you understand the word play in the headlines on *p.70*.

1 A popular toy for young children is *My Little Pony*.

2 At the end of a wedding ceremony the person in charge says 'I pronounce you man and wife'.

3 On gravestones you often see *R.I.P.* which means *Rest in peace*.

4 A *clone* is a genetic copy of an animal or plant.

5 The noise a dog makes is *woof*.

6 Metal starts to *rust* if you leave it outside in the rain

27 IT'S MY LIFE

English in use   Student A

Read the following and blame **B**.

You have just been on holiday leaving **B** to look after your flat.

You find the flat has been burgled because **B** forgot to close the bathroom window. Your tropical fish have died because **B** didn't feed them while you were away.

Your phone has been cut off because **B** didn't open the post and find the bill.

Defend yourself and make excuses when **B** blames you.

You are out on a drive in the country, the car has run out of petrol and you are lost in the middle of nowhere.

You don't have a map or a spare can of petrol.

You have forgotten your mobile phone and the number of the people you are supposed to be visiting.

Speak out

Read the interpretation of who you think is responsible for Stephanie's death. Agree or disagree.

Stephanie represents a traditional feminine role where women are passive and men dominate.

If you put Stephanie first there are two main reasons, according to whether you are a man or a woman. Men who put Stephanie first are usually macho and traditional. They believe that she deserved to die because she betrayed Cedric. Women who put Stephanie first reject the traditional subservient role of women in society and are likely to be committed feminists who accept individual responsibility for their destiny, i.e. Stephanie was responsible for the choices she made.

If you put her last you believe that women have no control over their own lives and are victims of chance and male domination.

The madman represents the relationship between individuals and society.

If you put the madman first then you believe in individual choice and responsibility. People are responsible for their own destiny so someone, even if mad, can exercise their free will.

If you put him last, then you believe that society is to blame and that he is just as much a victim as Stephanie. You believe that personality is determined by social surroundings and upbringing.

The taxi driver represents materialism and the love of money.

If you put the taxi driver first it means that you hate the material world and people who prize money. You are also likely to hate big business and the damage it does to the environment.

If you put the taxi driver last it means that you believe that the basic relationship human beings have with each other is economic. It was perfectly reasonable for the taxi driver to ask her to leave the car.

Cedric represents traditional male values, conservatism and conformity.

If you put Cedric first it means that you think he failed in his traditional male role as the protector of women. You are a strong believer in traditional male values.

If you put Cedric last you believe that it is not the responsibility of the male to take care of females.

Raymond represents individual freedom and self expression.

If you put Raymond first it means you are deeply conformist and disapprove of people who do not follow the crowd.

If you put him last you are likely to be an immature person. You are careless and irresponsible with other people's feelings, using your own 'freedom' as an excuse for your bad behaviour.

32 FOLLOW YOUR DREAM

Speak out   Student A

Describe your pictures to **B**. Work out the story between you.

02 PERSONAL PROFILES

Speak out   Student B

Read the text and complete the chart on *p.9*. Exchange information with **A**.

During the day Louise Wilkinson works as a children's librarian. But once the sun goes down she transforms herself into a vampire. Louise, 38, of London, has even got some fangs (vampire teeth). In her ten years as a vampire, she has collected a houseful of horror movie videos, skulls and bats. She enjoys being frightened, although she knows it is just a game. As secretary of the Dracula Society, which has 110 members, Louise has even been to Transylvania. She loves going to parties dressed as 'Elvira, Mistress of the Dark', where she pretends to bite the necks of the other guests. Sometimes she dresses up as one of Dracula's victims, and wears a white dress covered with artificial blood.

06 HAPPY TOGETHER

Speak out   Student B

Read the text and make notes under the headings on *p.20*.

Sark

Sark is one of the Channel Islands off the north west coast of France. It has been part of the British Isles since William the Conqueror conquered England in 1066. Most people have Norman ancestors. People speak French and English.

The Seigneur, or Lord, of Sark is the only person in the British Isles who can have his own army. No cars are allowed on the island. It is against the law for inhabitants to have female dogs or to keep pigeons. Only the Seigneur of Sark is allowed to keep pigeons.

13 GETTING THROUGH

Speak for yourself   Student B

Ask **A** for the telephone numbers of:

The Vatican	_____
Sydney Opera House	_____
The Kremlin	_____

Tell **A** the numbers of:

The White House	12 02 994 062
Buckingham Palace	44 171 403 604
The Hard Rock Cafe	17 18 865 016

Speak out   Student B

Situation 1

Your husband/wife has put an advertisement in the newspaper to try and sell some Labrador puppies. They can't come to the phone right now – invent some kind of excuse. You know some of the information but aren't clear about everything. You are fed up with getting so many calls so you aren't very friendly!

* The puppies are six weeks old.
* There are four black and four yellow ones. There are two males and two females of each colour. Homes have been found for some of the puppies but you're not exactly sure which ones.
* You think the puppies are about £150 each.
* They have a pedigree but as far as you know haven't been vaccinated.
* You're not sure when it will be possible to visit. You will have to take the caller's details so that your husband/wife can call back. Ask for a convenient time.

Situation 2

You are a travel agent and you have two old friends who own a hotel. You are ringing them up to check what has happened to a booking you have made. It is quite urgent as your customers are waiting for a reply. You have known the other couple for years. Ask about their news and business but try to keep the discussion short. You need to discuss the booking urgently. You are travelling around in your car at the moment and your mobile number is 0750 883309.

16 CATS AND RATS

Vocabulary   Group B

Check your definitions from *p.47*. Test a partner from Group **A**.

shift work	a job which involves working at different times of the day and night
go on strike	refuse to work usually because of low pay or poor working conditions

wages	the money you are paid for the job you do
full-time	for all the hours of the working week (usually about 40)
overtime	time spent at work after normal working hours

17 GOING PLACES

Speak out

Look at the photos. Agree on a holiday destination.

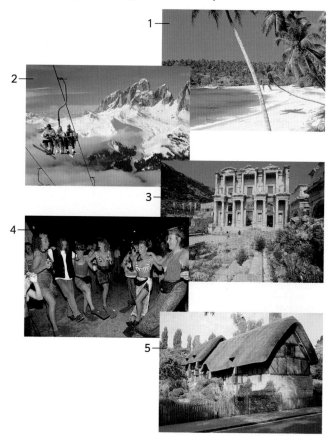

27 IT'S MY LIFE

English in use   Student B

Read the following and blame **A**.

You are out with **A** on a drive in the country.

The car has run out of petrol and you are lost in the middle of nowhere.

A hasn't brought a map or a spare can of petrol.

A also forgot the mobile phone and the number of the people you are supposed to be visiting.

Defend yourself and make excuses when **A** blames you.

You looked after **A**'s flat when they went on holiday. The flat was burgled because you didn't close the bathroom window.

The tropical fish died because you didn't feed them properly.

The phone has been cut off because you didn't open the post and find the bill.

32 FOLLOW YOUR DREAM

Speak out Student B

Describe your pictures to **A**. Work out the story between you.

06 HAPPY TOGETHER

Speak out Student C

Read the text and make notes under the headings on *p.20*.

Singapore

Singapore is an island state at the tip of the Malay peninsula. Its suburban train, the Mass Rapid Transport System, is perhaps the best in the world. The Chinese make up 76% of the population and Malays 15%. English is spoken by the Straits Chinese and the rest of the population speak Mandarin and Malay. Long-haired foreigners have to have their hair cut. You are not allowed to eat or drink on the metro or have a dirty car. You can't just go and buy a car. First of all you have to buy a certificate giving you permission at a monthly auction.

TAPESCRIPTS

01 YOURS INSINCERELY

Conversation 1

Marcel Victor, there's somebody I'd like you to meet. This is Fiona O' Doyle, she's over from Canada.

Fiona Pleased to meet you, Victor.

Victor Hi, Fiona. Would you like a glass of champagne?

Fiona Champagne, mm, yes please.

Victor So what brings you to London, Fiona?

Fiona Well, I'm a professional ice-skater ...

Victor An ice-skater. That's very interesting ...

Fiona ... and I'm in competition next week.

Victor A competition! So, Fiona, tell me, what's it like skating in front of all those people? It must be terrifying ...

Conversation 2

Bella Who is that woman in the awful dress who's coming towards us?

Alex That's Danielle Hearst, the artist. I've been trying to avoid her all evening.

Danielle Ah, there you are Alex, I've been looking for you everywhere.

Alex Danielle, it's been ages. You look wonderful.

Danielle Listen, I'd like to invite you to my exhibition this Friday evening.

Alex Friday evening? Oh Danielle, what a shame, I'm flying to Boston on Friday.

Danielle Oh dear, I was hoping you could come. Never mind.

Alex I'm so disappointed. I'm sure it'll be brilliant as usual.

Danielle Thanks. Anyway, it 's been lovely to see you, but I hope you'll excuse me, there's someone I must talk to ...

Alex Of course. Good luck on Friday, I'll be thinking of you.

Bella Her exhibition ... I can't stand her work!

Alex Neither can I ... Anyway, what are your plans for Friday?

Conversation 3

Bill Is that the time? I didn't realize it was so late. I really must be going.

Carole Do you have to go so early, Bill?

Bill I'm afraid so, I've got an early start tomorrow.

Carole I'm sorry you can't stay longer.

Bill So am I. I've had a wonderful time. You know, I don't usually enjoy parties.

Carole Neither do I ... but this has been so different, Bill.

Bill Yes it has. I hope we can get together again soon.

Carole Mm, so do I. I tell you what, why don't I give you my number?

02 PERSONAL PROFILES

Saskia Goodness. They look lovely in this glass case. I've never seen so many ... There must be forty or so.

Justin Actually, I've got a lot more which I don't display. I've got ninety-eight altogether.

Saskia Wow ... So how long have you been collecting them, Justin?

Justin For at least eleven or twelve years, I suppose.

Saskia Oh really! And what made you start?

Justin Well, I used to travel a lot with my job. The first time I bought one was in a shop at Frankfurt airport. They really caught my eye and I ended up buying one of those transparent ones with different coloured hands. About twelve years ago I think it was. I was feeling, you know, a bit fed up and I thought they were bright and cheerful so ...

Saskia ... you bought one to cheer yourself up?

Justin Yeah, that's about it. And that's how I got started!

Saskia Wow. And do you actually wear them?

Justin Mm, yeah, depending on my mood. Though sometimes it's hard to choose.

Saskia I bet ... Just look at all these types. I thought they were all pretty much the same, but it's the first time I've seen these ones here.

Justin   That's right, 'cos they're the, er, special editions. This one is a particular favourite of mine. It was designed by Christian Lacroix, and as you can see, instead of having hands, there's a dot on that disc, which moves around slowly. I just love the jewels on the face as well.

Saskia   So where do you, erm, pick them all up?

Justin   Well, ever since I got really hooked I've had to go after them specially.

Saskia   Specially?

Justin   Yeah, erm, people queue up for twenty-four hours to get a new edition, especially at Christmas. It's worth it because if you get one for £100, chances are you'll be able to sell it for £500 a few months later. I don't do that often any more though …

Saskia   Amazing. And what's the most expensive one you've ever bought?

Justin   I hate to think; I paid £1,000 for a rare one another collector had, but that's nothing. I've heard of collectors paying up to £50,000 for watches if, say, they have been designed by a well-known designer for a really famous person.

Saskia   Wow. I hope they're well insured. And which one is your favourite?

Justin   Usually the one I've just bought. Just look at this one, it's only the second time it has been out of its box … yes, that blue one with the pictures of watch parts on the strap and that pretty star on the second hand … Isn't it lovely?

03   FIXING YOU UP

Part A

Archie's second wife, Janet, talks about her relationship with Archie.

'Well, we worked together. It wasn't exactly love at first sight, 'cos well, for one thing he was married at the time, and he was my boss, and to tell you the truth we didn't really get on with each other very well. He was really, you know, a very serious boss, and business-like and so on. Anyway, um, I left for another job and then I bumped into him a couple of, um, three years later, by which time he and his wife had split up; um, they'd been separated for a couple of years but not yet divorced. Anyway, when he asked me out for a drink I was absolutely astonished! A date with my old boss, but I said yes 'cos I felt sorry for him.

At first we were a bit suspicious of each other, but, um, one thing led to another … Um, I think we were both amazed when we found ourselves living together. We didn't even introduce each other to our families for ages. People who knew both of us couldn't believe it. They said, um, you know, that we would be the last people in the world they'd ever put together.

It was only after we'd been together for years that we decided to formalize things. And when we did, it was, you know, very low-key and quiet in a registry office with just a few friends and family round at the flat afterwards. It's seventeen years and two kids later now, and so far, touch wood, it's worked out really well. Personally, I think everyone ought to live together first. People should never rush into marriage.'

Part B

Archie's friend Jacob talks about Archie's marriage to his first wife, Linda.

'Oh, er, yes, I definitely think you can get married too young, you know. Take Archie and Linda for instance.

I introduced him to her at a party when we were all students together. Everyone could see they really fancied each other and they started going out together.

After we graduated they stayed together, um, and I think there was quite a lot of pressure, you know, um, from her parents, for them to get married. So they got engaged and they had the usual church wedding and bridesmaids and stuff. People said they looked a perfect couple. I was best man … but I just knew they were wrong for each other.

The moment they tried to settle down the rows started. I think, um, part of the reason was they came from different backgrounds; she was from a very well off family and was quite spoilt and Archie didn't live up to her expectations. Anyway, er, in the end she met someone else and that was that. I wasn't surprised when they broke up. Luckily there were no kids. Personally, I think it was best for both of them. People should think hard before they marry. They say that opposites attract, but do they stay together? Oh, another thing is, they ought to do what suits them and not take too much notice of what family and other people say.'

05   HOME TOWN

Speaker 1   beautiful temples, smiling people, pollution, traffic jams

Speaker 2   exciting nightlife, yellow cabs, people in a hurry, Broadway musicals, the homeless

Speaker 3   quiet suburbs, crowded underground, a sandwich in the park, late night shopping, red bus to the station

Speaker 4   beach volleyball, fantastic scenery, beautiful people, Carnival, dangerous after dark

Part A

Diana   Well, there's California on the west coast, and then Nevada is next to that, and then Utah's next to that … so it's west … The Rocky Mountains run right down from Canada down to, into, Latin America actually, and the eastern part of Utah is the Rocky Mountains.

Julian   Is there actually a 'salt lake' there?

Diana   Yes. There's, let me see, on one side of Salt Lake City is the Rocky Mountains, and on the other side, the Great Salt Lake itself; it used to be a great big sea, and it's just shrunk down to a lake now. Salt Lake City is in a basin, like a big valley.

Part B

Julian   Oh right. And what was Salt Lake City like to grow up in?

Diana   Well, when I was growing up it used to be … it was kind of assumed that everybody was Mormon. It's changed a lot since then; it's gotten a lot bigger, a lot more, erm, cosmopolitan I guess, if you like …

Julian   What was there to do when you were a kid?

Diana   Lots of things, I used to go to church, and, and there was a camp in the summer, and I dunno, all the usual things kids do.

Julian   Oh right, summer camp. And is it still very much a Mormon city?

Diana   It's getting less and … well … no … yeah, yeah it is … it still is. It's getting more cosmopolitan all the time. But the outskirts, around the city, are more Mormon.

Part C

Julian   What do people do for a living? Er, is there any industry there?

Diana   You bet, there's a big copper mine, and, er, recently there's been a lot of big businesses, big companies, moving their headquarters, their organizations to Salt Lake, 'cos the labour is highly educated, but salaries are a lot lower than in California. American Express has their headquarters there, and there are a lot of really big Mormon-owned companies, like IBM. IBM is Mormon-owned.

Julian   Oh, is it? And does it help if you're a Mormon?

Diana   To get a job?

Julian   Yeah.

Diana   No. I don't think so. Not any more. Not these days.

Part D

Julian   What is there to do?

Diana   Well we have skiing in the north of the state. I went on holiday there just a few months ago.

Julian   Oh, did you?

Diana   Yeah, it was wonderful … And in the south we have the Canyon Lands.

Julian   The Canyon Lands. Is that where the Indians are?

Diana   Native Americans? Yeah, there are native Americans, they're Navaho, they're down in the south, in Monument Valley.

Julian   Monument Valley?

Diana   Yeah, you must've seen 'em in westerns. These pillars of rock, they just come straight up, erm, out of the ground, like, erm, long fingers.

Julian   Oh, right. Now I know. And now that you live in San Francisco do you miss any of this?

Diana   Sure. I miss the desert in the south, I miss the canyons, but I like to go back there fairly regularly, 'cos of family …

Julian   Would you like to go back, you know, for good one day?

Diana   Mm. Maybe one day, but not right now. San Francisco is where I wanna be for the time being.

06   HAPPY TOGETHER

Part 1

Tricia and Larry are talking about *Celebration*.

Tricia   What is the great attraction of *Celebration*, Larry?

Larry   Simple. City life's hell these days. There are security guards in schools and kids shooting each other. People want to be part of a real community again. There's a lot of nostalgia for small town living, you know, for the time when you didn't need to worry if your kids were playing in the street.

Tricia   I see. So who can live there, in *Celebration* then, is it just for the rich?

Larry   No, not at all, there's a real social and ethnic mix. There are different styles and sizes of house according to your means and the size of your family.

Tricia   Do you think it'll work?

Larry   Who knows, but it'll be interesting to see how the first generation grows up.

Tricia   It must be like living in the 50s.

Larry   Yeah, but don't forget it's a modern town too.

Tricia   A modern town? How do you mean?

Larry   Well, all of the homes are 'online', you know, connected by computer. And there're facilities like a boating lake, a golf course, you name it. And all for 20,000 people.

Part 2

Tricia	Is it difficult to move there, you know, is there a lot of competition?
Larry	For sure. People are desperate to change their quality of life. But you have to agree to respect a certain number of rules too ...
Tricia	Rules, like what?
Larry	Things like, er, curtains. The ones facing the street are supposed to be white. They mustn't be any other colour.
Tricia	Oh, really!
Larry	... 'n another thing is, you're not supposed to fix your car in the street. You've got to do it out of sight, in your garage.
Tricia	That's fair enough, I guess.
Larry	Yeah, I think so. Oh, and another thing is that you can design your house but you've got to choose the basic style from a book ... If you ever want to make a change you're supposed to get the approval of the architects.
Tricia	But that's the same in lots of places, isn't it? I mean, personally, I'd far rather have some regulations than a free-for-all.
Larry	I almost forgot. There's one other thing. They won't let you have palm trees in your garden.
Tricia	No palm trees! Now, that is weird.

07 POLITENESS PAYS

1

Man	Do you think I could borrow your dictionary this weekend?
Woman	Sorry, normally I'd say yes, but I'm going to need it myself.

2

Woman	Is it all right if I smoke in here?
Man	Well actually, I don't think you're allowed to.

3

Woman 1	Does anyone mind if I open the window?
Woman 2	Well, I'd rather you didn't if you don't mind. I'm a bit cold.

4

Woman	Excuse me. Do you happen to have change for five pounds?
Man	I'm afraid not, I've just used all my change for the phone box.

5

Man	I was wondering if you could spare me a minute to look at this form.
Woman	Yes, of course, let's go into my office, shall we?

6

Woman	Do you mind if I borrow your paper?
Man	No, of course not, I've already read it.

7

Woman	Would it be possible to move to that table in the shade?
Waiter	I'm afraid that table is reserved, madam, but I'll see what I can do.

8

Teacher	Jenny and Samantha, excuse me for interrupting, but could you possibly continue your fascinating conversation after the lesson?
Girls	Oh, sorry, Mr Burton.

08 AS I REMEMBER

a

Well, there were good and bad times; I think one of the worst was when we had physics tests. We used to have one at the end of each term. We had to memorize this thing called 'the Archimedes Principle'. Anyway, we had the test and my mind went blank. I couldn't remember a thing. The teacher, she'd get really angry for nothing at all, you know, well, she was furious, she made me write it out fifty times.

b

I can never walk past that old war memorial without blushing. You see, it takes me back to when I had my first date. All the children would wait for each other there and then they would go to the cinema or something; it was the place, I'll never know why. I'm sure that if you ask lots of the people round here of my generation they'll say it reminds them of the same thing.

c

I think one of the most important decisions I ever made was when I got the envelope offering me the place to study economics at university. I'll always remember opening the letter, and the feeling of relief mixed with disappointment. Relief, because someone actually wanted me, but disappointment because I knew in my heart of hearts it wasn't what I wanted. I decided not to go, went travelling for a year, and studied languages instead.

d

'Don't forget to write,' she'd said as I left. It was quite an experience going away for a year. Anyway, I kept my promise and remembered to write every week for the time I was away. I would always send a few photos too. A few weeks ago she gave all the letters back to me, together with an album of all the photographs I'd sent her. It's a marvellous souvenir to have; sometimes I just take them out of my box and I can remember the faces and places all those years ago.

e

My earliest memory? Trying to push my pram down the stairs; it was when I was, er, I must have only been about two. It was even before I could talk but somehow I still remember it vividly. I used to be quite adventurous then. Anyway, I fell from the top of the stairs to the bottom.

09 IT HAPPENED TO ME

Part 1

Julian	While we're on the subject ... I'll never forget something that happened to me when I went hitch-hiking one summer. I'd just left school and I thought I'd travel round Europe for a bit.
Sue	What, on your own?
Julian	No, I was with a friend called Tony. Anyway, we had been down to Greece and were making our way back, and had almost run out of money, when someone picked us up in Germany and took us all the way to the middle of France. He even put us up for the night.
Alan	That was lucky.
Julian	Yeah, the trouble was, though, that he lived in a village in the middle of nowhere. After breakfast he dropped us off at the main road and we said goodbye. Unfortunately, there were hardly any cars on the road.
Alan	Oh no.

Part 2

Julian	Anyway, finally this gorgeous car, a BMW I think it was, stopped, and the driver, a Dutch guy, said that he was heading north right past the channel ports to Holland.
Sue	That was a bit of luck.
Julian	We couldn't believe it ... but it turned out to be a huge mistake. At first we enjoyed travelling in luxury and the driver was really chatty. But by the evening he could hardly keep his eyes open.
Alan	Really. How come?
Julian	Well, apparently, he had been driving all through the night and had picked us up for someone to talk to.
Sue	He must have been tired.
Julian	Tired? He was exhausted. But would he stop driving? Oh no, he just kept going on and on. I had run out of subjects of conversation and was busy watching the road.
Alan	So what did you do?
Julian	Well, nothing! I didn't want to show I was scared. Anyway, about ten o'clock that evening the inevitable happened; we were coming up to a roundabout and he fell asleep just for a second ... we hit a lorry ... the doors burst open ...
Sue	How awful! You must have been really scared.
Julian	Scared! I was absolutely terrified! I was shaking like a leaf. And when I looked around for Tony, he wasn't in the car ...
Sue	Was he hurt?
Julian	... but then we heard laughter and there he was, on the floor between the seats; he was covered in coats and sleeping bags.
Alan	And was he OK?
Julian	Yeah, he even thought it was a huge joke. It's put me off hitch-hiking for ever, though ...
Sue	I'm not surprised ... you know, this reminds me of something similar that happened to me ...

11 HIGHLY RECOMMENDED

1

Elaine	We saw a great film the other night at the Picture Palace. Have you seen *The Commitments*?
Penny	No, I've heard it's good though. What's it about?
Elaine	Well, it's, erm, set in Dublin, and about a group of young people who form a soul music band, and they call themselves *The Commitments*. The story's great. You really get involved with the characters, especially when the relationships turn sour. It's extremely funny too. But the best bit's the music. It's fantastic. All the old hits. You really should see it, it's absolutely brilliant.
Dave	Are you talking about that awful film *The Commitments*? I wouldn't bother if I were you!

2

Andrew	Have you read anything good recently?
Sylvie	Well, have you tried *Captain Corelli's Mandolin* yet?
Andrew	No, I read about it in the paper, but the title put me off. It doesn't sound like my sort of thing.
Sylvie	Oh no. It's the best book I've read for ages.
Andrew	Yeah? Tell me about it.

Sylvie Well, it's a kind of mixture of a war story and a love story rolled into one. It takes place during the Second World War and is set on a Greek island. The main character is this Italian officer called Antonio Corelli, from the title.

Andrew Mm, sounds intriguing.

Sylvie It is, it's absolutely gripping. I couldn't put it down. It's a bitter-sweet story, at the beginning it's a sparkling comedy, but eventually it turns to tragedy.

Andrew And does it end happily?

Sylvie Well, I don't want to spoil it for you. You must read it for yourself. I can lend it to you if you like.

3

Paul We discovered a wonderful Indian restaurant called *Vijays* in Kilburn the other evening.

Judith Oh yes? Whereabouts is it?

Paul Just off the High Road.

Judith Really. I've never heard of it.

Paul I know, Dave told me about it. We went for my birthday. It doesn't look much from the outside but the food's really tasty, especially the starters, and the service is really attentive.

Judith What did you have?

Paul To begin with I had a sort of crispy pancake with coconut sauce.

Judith Stop, you're making my mouth water.

Paul Well, you should try it.

12 IT HAPPENED TO ME

1 A travel agent tells you that the flight you want to take is full. Say it doesn't matter, and that you'll go on the following flight.

2 You are on a train but you would like to listen to a football match on the radio. Ask the other passengers for permission. Promise to keep the volume low.

3 The driver of the car you are in is reversing into a side street. Warn him that there are children playing.

4 You are in a restaurant but can't decide what to have. Ask the waiter for his suggestions.

5 You couldn't find a very important document. You were going mad with worry. In the end you found it. Tell the story.

6 Someone asks you why you're looking so concerned. Tell them you have a lot of personal problems.

7 A friend wants to invest all her money in a risky business. She asks for your honest opinion.

8 You are organizing a day trip. Your colleague says that the place you are planning to visit is expensive. Agree, but suggest taking a picnic to keep the cost down.

13 GETTING THROUGH

1 01189 342 0098

2 018862 99 4134

3 00 33 2 47 734290

4 0800 772555

Conversation 1

Karen Mr Blakemore's office, Karen speaking.

Rona Good morning, could I speak to Mr Blakemore, please?

Karen May I ask who's calling?

Rona Yes, my name's Rona Cash, I'm a reporter from the Essex Messenger.

Karen I see, and can I ask what it's in connection with?

Rona Well, it's regarding the new shopping centre; I was wondering if he could discuss some questions about the plans.

Karen If you'd like to hold the line for a moment, I'll see if he's available …

Karen Hello, Miss Cash. I'm afraid he's going to be busy all morning.

Rona OK, when would be a good time for me to call again?

Karen Well, I'm not quite sure but, um, if you'd like to give me your details I'll make sure he calls you back.

Rona Certainly, thank you very much. It's Rona, that's R-O-N-A …

Conversation 2

Damien Hello, 'Designs on You'.

Paul Is that Damien?

Damien Speaking. Who's this?

Paul It's Paul Walsh here.

Damien Paul, hi! I didn't recognize your voice. So, what can I do for you?

Paul It's Candy. I really need to speak to her. Is she in?

Damien Candy? Hang on a minute. I'll see if she's around … Hi, Paul. Sorry, she is in, but she's tied up with a client. Do you want to leave a message?

Paul Yeah … I, erm, no, it's too complicated. It's about the cover design. There are still a few things we need to sort out.

Damien OK, I'll get her to give you a ring the moment she's free. Has she got your number?

Paul Good point. I'm on my mobile. I'd better give it to you anyway.

Damien Just a moment, let me find a pen that works. Right, fire away.

14 INTO THE FUTURE

a

Father Get off that wall straight away, Martin. You're going to break your neck one day. Boys are all the same, aren't they?

b

Tony Would you like to come for drinks at the weekend?

Jan Oh, I'd love to, but I'm looking after a colleague from Boston.

Tony Oh, bad luck. Some other time, then?

c

Waiter Are you ready to order?

Charles Right, decision time. I'll have the steak with the Roquefort sauce. What about you, Sandra?

Sandra Mm, I think I'll have the same. Oh no, don't look, but there's Melanie. I think she's seen us.

Melanie Hello, you two. You won't mind if I join you. Have you ordered yet? I'm absolutely starving.

Sandra We've already ordered; we're both having the steak.

Melanie Mm, that sounds delicious … let's have a quick look at the menu …

d

Businessman Could you tell me the times of trains to Cambridge?

Clerk Yes, they leave on the hour every other hour. And the next one goes in two minutes.

Businessman Two minutes!

Clerk Yes, if you hurry you might just get it. Platform nine, pay on the train.

Businessman Platform nine? Thanks.

Clerk I'll be surprised if he makes it with that heavy bag.

e

Presenter So, the outlook for the holiday weekend is rather unsettled, I'm afraid. If we look at the weather map for Saturday morning we can see that it is going to be a wet and windy day for most of the region. There might be a few sunny periods in the afternoon but don't count on it. The bad weather will clear on Sunday morning, though, and hopefully Sunday evening and the bank holiday Monday will be dry.

1 This is Gwen Morris's answering machine. I'm not able to come to the phone right now, but if you'd like to leave a message please do so after the beep and I'll get back to you as soon as possible.

Michael Gwen, hi, it's Michael here. I'm just ringing to say that I'll be arriving tomorrow evening – that's Friday – at Heathrow at around six thirty. The flight's bound to be delayed 'cos of the weather this end, but even so, expect to see me around nineish. Don't bother to make anything, will you, 'cos I'll have eaten on the plane. Anyway, I'm really looking forward to seeing you. Till tomorrow then. Bye.

2 **Tessa** It's Tessa from the garage here. The 'child seat' you ordered is due to arrive later on this morning. Joe'll be fitting it after lunch and it shouldn't take him too long. I'd say it's likely to be ready by round about three; he'll've done it by then. Perhaps we'd better say fourish though, just to be safe.

15 DRESS FOR SUCCESS

So, let's go over the key points again. First of all, clothes. A week or so before the interview, go to the place of work and look carefully at how they dress. You want to make sure that you look as though you belong to the 'tribe', you know, wear the right kind of 'uniform'. Select the clothes from your wardrobe that match the look you want. If you need to buy some new clothes then get used to wearing them so that you don't feel too awkward and self-conscious.

Now, the right clothes are important, but think of your facial appearance too. Get rid of things like earrings and pony tails if you're a man, and shave off the beard - mentioning no names, Richard - 'cos if there's one thing lots of interviewers hate, it's beards. Don't eat onions, garlic, or curry for at least two days before an interview; you don't want to kill them with your breath, do you?

Right, now for the interview. Remember that you probably win or lose that job in the first thirty seconds. You never get a second chance to make a good first impression! Walk in confidently and look as though you're really looking forward to the experience. Try not to look miserable or scared, and – if it's offered – shake the interviewer's hand firmly. If there's a row of interviewers behind a table, look everyone in the eye to show that you're confident. When you sit down, sit up straight, and don't lie back in the chair, or even worse have your hands behind your head. Keep both feet on the ground, and keep your hands open and relaxed on your lap, whatever you do, don't play with your hair or keys. Don't cross your arms or legs. Why? Yes, that's right; no negative body language!

As for the questions, try to be honest. If you try to sound too perfect they'll know you're lying! Interviewers love to ask about your negative points or what the problem was with your last job. Never, ever criticize your past employers or boss; it's the kiss of death. If someone asks you an awkward question, try not to look daggers at them. Try and turn a negative point into something positive, like 'Well, I think I was a bit too enthusiastic in my last job; I see now that I got on my colleagues' nerves a little', and so on. It'll show that you have matured and are ready to learn ...

a   What kind of leadership qualities do you have?
    Well, when I was a student I was in charge of a group of young people at a summer camp, and, as you know, adolescents can be very difficult to lead.

b   Do you have any skills or hobbies you think might be useful for this job?
    I speak French and German, I think that could be extremely useful, and I love anything to do with history.

c   What do you think is your greatest fault?
    That's a difficult question. Sometimes I can get impatient with colleagues who work too slowly.

d   How do you feel about spending time away from home?
    Nobody likes to do it but if it's part of the job I suppose you just have to make the most of it.

e   Why did you leave your last job?
    I was replacing someone who was on maternity leave, so my contract ended when she came back.

f   What makes you think you could do this job?
    I think I've got the right background and personal qualities to do the job.

g   Tell me something you're proud of.
    Winning the 'Employee of the month' competition three times in one year.

h   What do you see yourself doing in five years' time? I'm not really sure ... Maybe I'd like to have my own business.

17   GOING PLACES

Barbara   Yes, let's look at the brochure, shall we?
John   Right then. Mm. So, what do you think?
Barbara   Well, it all looks fairly interesting, but I think the Southern Tour's better 'cos you don't go to so many places.
John   Well, that's a funny reason. I thought the idea was to get to know the country.
Barbara   Yes, but I don't fancy spending all my time in a coach.
John   Yeah, but the Baltic Tour goes to Gdansk and so on ...
Barbara   I suppose so, but my view of Gdansk is that it's a pretty industrial place – I'm not that keen on spending my holiday there.

John   ... and there's also this castle, the one of the Teutonic knights.
Barbara   Mm, it does sound interesting. I dunno, I'd love to see that, but it just sounds too much, know what I mean?
John   Don't you think the first one spends too long in Cracow?
Barbara   Not really, you could easily spend several days there. I think I'd rather know one or two places well, rather than rush about all over the place. These visits to the amber workshops could be fascinating too.
John   I know what you mean, but what about going up to the mountains, to Zakopane? I've heard there are beautiful wooden houses and – look at these photos – the scenery's beautiful!
Barbara   I must say, I'm not that keen, I've heard it's a bit touristy. But if you really want to go, there's a full-day excursion from Cracow.
John   Um, that's a thought. I could go on that while you went shopping, I suppose. There's a trip to Auschwitz too. I'm not sure if I really feel up to that, though.
Barbara   I know what you mean, but I think it's the kind of thing everyone should see.
John   Yeah, maybe. Otherwise, I could visit this salt mine instead. Given the choice I'd prefer to do that.
Barbara   I tell you something though, I understand what you're saying about the Baltic tour, this one that goes everywhere. It sounds the most interesting, but I think the pace would be exhausting.
John   Yeah, we'd need another holiday to get over it. I could do with more of a rest. Tell you what though, we could always do our own thing.
Barbara   Yes, I was starting to think that. Why don't we get our own flights over, say, to Cracow, and then hire a car?
John   Hire a car? Um, you're right. It'd be more flexible, but I bet it works out more expensive. How about giving them a ring and finding out what's possible?
Barbara   OK, we'd better do it straightaway then, 'cos as usual we've left everything very late.

18   ALL THE BEST

Marina   What's the worst place you've ever stayed in?
Tamsin   The worst place I've ever stayed in? That's easy. It was called the White Horse Hotel, a couple of years ago. It had been recommended in a guide book so we thought it would be all right and so we just took the room without checking it out. Anyway, the hotel looked really quite nice, the reception and everything, and it was quite expensive.
Marina   So what was wrong with it then?
Tamsin   Well, to begin with, when we went to bed, the bed was awful, we just rolled into the middle, and it managed to be extremely soft but lumpy at the same time. And the other thing was the bathroom. The smell was awful, it stank ...
Marina   Yuk!
Tamsin   And it just got worse and worse as the night went on. I think it must have been the drains or something.
Marina   Couldn't you have opened the windows?

Tamsin   Well, we tried but we were on quite a busy road, you see, so it was noisy too.
Marina   Oh, right.
Tamsin   Anyway, the following morning we couldn't get away fast enough, even though we'd said we wanted to stay for two nights.
Marina   And did you complain or anything?
Tamsin   I did, yes, I wrote a letter to the manager, and do you know, they offered us a free extra night!

19   SO MANY QUESTIONS

1   I wonder if you could tell me which party you voted for at the last election?
    Mm ... Now that would be telling, wouldn't it?

2   So how much do you weigh then?
    I haven't got a clue. I've got absolutely no idea!

3   Next, I'd like you to tell me what your favourite book is.
    My favourite book? To be honest, I've never really thought about it.

4   Now, I'd like to know who would look after your child if it was sick.
    I'd prefer not to answer that, if you don't mind.

5   Do you believe in angels?
    Goodness. That's a very interesting question. I'll have to think about that.

6   ... and finally, would you mind telling me how much you earn?
    That's a rather personal question. If you don't mind I'd rather not say.

7   Have you ever been in trouble with the police?
    Mind your own business!

8   Do you think you could tell me what you'd change about your appearance?
    I haven't the faintest idea! What would you change?

21   FESTIVAL

Part 1

Right then, I'm going to tell you a little bit about the festival of *Hina Matsuri*. I think this was one of the most interesting and touching things I witnessed while I was living in Japan. It's a one-day festival, and takes place in Japan each year on 3rd March. *Hina Matsuri* means 'little doll' and it is, as you can probably guess, a festival which is completely dedicated to dolls. Many Japanese girls take part in the festival.

Part 2

Now these dolls aren't something that you just play with, like a Barbie or something like that, rather, they are something that you display, you know, have on show. I've brought a couple in, and you can see just how beautiful they are. They are dressed in the most exquisite costumes. Lots and lots of girls are given a set of dolls when they are born, often by their, er, grandparents, or else there are dolls which have been in the family for generations. The idea is that the dolls are used to teach the girls about traditional values. They take enormous care of them.

Part 3

Anyway, in the week leading up to *Hina Matsuri*, families put the dolls in the best room of the house. They take a great deal of pride in the display. Incidentally, the dolls have to be put away after *Hina Matsuri*, otherwise it brings bad luck. If you're ever lucky enough to be invited, you'll probably be offered rice cakes called *mochi*. They're beautifully wrapped up in cherry blossom leaves. You see, this kind of perfection is just taken for granted in Japan. The cakes are offered to the dolls and then to the visitors.

Part 4

I've said something about the private side of the festival but now I'd like to talk about its public side. Some Japanese people believe you can transfer illness or bad luck to one of these dolls. So, for instance, someone with a sick child might give a doll to a temple. As you can see, this one has got hundreds and hundreds. Anyway, what happens is, the dolls are put into boats and taken down to the sea by people wearing traditional costumes and robes. There, priests say prayers, and the boats are sent out to sea. You see, the idea is, of course, that any bad luck or illness is taken away with the dolls. Over the years it has become an extremely popular sight, and more and more people come each year to watch the ceremony. It really is quite a moving occasion.

23 A GOLDEN AGE

Part A

Good afternoon, everyone. I'd like to welcome you to the Forge Mill Needle Museum. My name's Sue, and I'm going to give you a tour of the mill. First of all, I'm going to tell you a little bit about this site and put needle-making in its historical context. Right, so originally it was the Moors of Spain who invented the needle-making process. But the technique didn't get to England until the 1600s. This mill began some time in the eighteenth century. Before that there used to be a blacksmith's forge on this site. The water wheel that we can hear in the background provided the power for the blacksmiths, and later, for the mill. Now, if you'd all like to follow me, um, I'll take you down to the exhibition. Watch yourselves here now, be careful of the low ceiling ...

Part B

All right. Is everyone here? I'd now like to tell you something about the stages of needle-making. Workers were used to making the needles by hand in their homes. In fact, they had little direct contact with the factory, which they called 'The Fountain' after the name of the pub where they got their materials. They used to bring back their finished work here, to the mill, for cleaning and polishing. By the end of the 1800s, three million needles a week were finished here, and the town of Redditch was the needle capital of the world. Now, if you'd like to come this way...

Part C

Right, let me tell you a bit about the manufacturing process. So, how were needles actually made then? We're standing now in front of the models which show exactly how. In order to make the needles, they started with long lengths of wire. Their first job was to make the wire the right thickness and it was pulled through a series of holes of different sizes until it was exactly right. After that, they had to cut the wire into short lengths with a pair of enormous scissors; over here you can see some. The next job was to put the points on the needles, a special skill called 'pointing'.

Part D

Pointing took place here, in this mill, in the 1800s. Please gather round. I'd like to draw your attention to this model of a pointer who's sharpening needles. It was an extremely dangerous job. New pointers had to quickly get used to working in dusty, noisy conditions with hardly any light. People often got hurt, and clothes caught fire. One poor man who jumped into the river to put out the flames even drowned.

However, it was the metal dust that they breathed in that was the real killer. And what has our pointer got to protect himself? Just this piece of cloth over his mouth. Pointers got six times the average wage, but can you guess what their life expectancy was? About eight years only! It was a scandal; Charles Dickens even wrote about it ...

24 THE WAY TO DO IT

1

Marc	Pamela, can you show me how to back up a file onto this disk?
Pamela	No problem, which file do you want to copy?
Marc	This one, 'English homework'.
Pamela	OK, have you got the disk? Right, first of all you put it into the drive, here. That's right. Now if you look you can see that the icon has come up on the screen here.
Marc	Oh yeah.
Pamela	Now, with the mouse, you move the cursor across and click on the file, just once, and keep your finger down, now drag it over to the disk icon. OK, great. Now if you let go it should copy. There you are. Afterwards, go up to the 'Special' menu and select 'Eject Disk'; and there you are.
Marc	Great, thanks!

2

Mr Tyler	Jenny, could you come here a moment?
Jenny	Oh no, not again! Yes, Mr Tyler.
Mr Tyler	I can't send this message. Can you show me what to do again?
Jenny	Right, let's have a look, shall we? So, first of all put the sheet of paper in the top here. No, you've, erm, got it round the wrong way ... no, no, turn it upside down.
Mr Tyler	What, with the text facing downwards?
Jenny	Yeah, 'cos the machine has to scan the document, to copy what's written on it.
Mr Tyler	Oh, I see.
Jenny	Now dial the number. That noise, it means that you're connected. Now, you see the button marked 'Send'? Press that, and the document should go through. There you are. Easy!
Mr Tyler	I don't think I'll ever get the hang of it.

3

Dad	I put the match on this tape, just after a wild-life programme about foxes.
Justin	Right, where's the remote control?
Dad	There on the sofa; OK, fast forward a bit. Stop. Let's have a look. Press 'Play' ... Almost there, it's just after the adverts. Now pause it while I get the beers.
Justin	I'm really looking forward to this ... hold on, what's this then, it's a gardening programme.
Dad	Oh no, I think I must have recorded the wrong channel.
Justin	Honestly, Dad, I don't believe it, all you had to do was scan the bar code from the TV magazine.

4

Tourist	Oh excuse me, is this machine out of order? I can't get it to accept my card.
Passer-by	I don't think so, would you like me to help you?
Tourist	Thanks, that's really kind of you.
Passer-by	OK, first of all, put your cashcard in the slot, no, not that way, you need to put it in the other way round, with the black stripe facing downwards.
Tourist	Oh I see.
Passer-by	And now key in your PIN number, you know, your personal code. I promise you I'm not looking. And then press 'Enter', the green button. Fine, OK, now choose how much you want to withdraw with the buttons on the side, and now 'Enter' again, and here comes your cash, and the card. Voilà!
Tourist	Thank you very much, I'm much obliged.
Passer-by	You're welcome.

5

Jim	Have you used one of these before?
Daphne	No, never.
Jim	Right, first of all, look through the viewfinder. Is it comfortable like that? That's the picture you'll get. OK so far?
Daphne	Yes, fine.
Jim	Right. Now, at the moment it says 'stand-by', which means it's ready to record. So simply press the red button to start. What can you see now?
Daphne	It says 'recording' and there's a light flashing on and off.
Jim	That's great.
Daphne	Do I have to focus it?
Jim	No, it does it automatically, but you can zoom in and out by using this button with the arrows.
Daphne	And afterwards, when I've finished?
Jim	Just press the red button again, then turn the machine off using the on-off switch at the side.

25 INSTANT OPINIONS

Article 1: My little cloney

Ross	Honestly, this is just too much, I find this really creepy. Of course it's fine for a child to have a pretty doll, but it's quite another thing for it to look exactly like her. There's something unhealthy about it. It's a bit like one of those horror movies, isn't it, you know, when the doll comes to life and starts murdering everyone. Oof.
Cathy	Mm, I think they're absolutely gorgeous ... so cute. My daughter's really into this sort of thing, you know dressing up her dolls in her old baby clothes and stuff, and I just know that she'd love something like this. They must cost a fortune though.
Emma	I've heard about these dolls, yes, but there's something sinister about them, don't you think? According to this article I read, it's a toy for adults rather than kids. I mean, you know this is a child that's never going to be naughty or get itself dirty. Spooky!

Article 2: I pronounce you man and woof

Ross	The poor things. All dressed up like that. It's so unfair. It's like dogs having psychiatrists. I think it's absolutely crazy. Animals don't have emotions like humans. As far as I'm concerned dogs are dogs and people are people. I blame the owners, these weddings are just a fashion, aren't they? They think it's the thing to do, but it's complete nonsense.
Cathy	I suppose they look quite sweet all dressed up and everything, but really I think it's a waste of time and money. In my opinion they could've done something much more worthwhile with what they've spent.

Emma What a terrible idea, it's absolutely appalling, don't you think? I don't believe in pretending that animals are like humans. Personally, I think they shouldn't be allowed. I guess it's just a matter of time, though, before we see them over here.

Article 3: Rust in peace

Ross I think it's great. It's like Viking chiefs going out to sea in a burning boat, isn't it? I'm sure some people don't approve, but he's been buried the way he wanted, that's the main thing. So yeah, why not?

Cathy On one level I think it's great to do your own thing, but on another, I think 'how awful'. I don't know how I'd feel if I had a loved one in that cemetery – it robs it of dignity rather, doesn't it? All things considered, it's not a good idea.

Emma How weird! It's certainly different, but the thing is, I could see it quickly becoming abused, you know, people being buried in old telephone boxes or wrapped up like Egyptian mummies, where would it all stop?

26 THE BIGGEST HOAX OF ALL?

Part A

Miriam What's that you're reading?
Martin It's about the, erm, moon landings, you know in 1969, about how they didn't really happen.
Miriam Oh no. Not another weird theory!
Martin You can laugh, but the evidence is really convincing.

Part B

Miriam Go on then.
Martin Well, to begin with, their space suits wouldn't have protected them. The astronauts would have died of radiation, been fried alive ...
Miriam Really?
Martin Yes, really ... And the other big thing is, they wouldn't all have been able to get into the capsule 'cos there just wasn't enough room for them.
Miriam But what about all the photos and films?
Martin Faked, every one of them, by the US government.
Miriam Faked?
Martin Yup. Just look at the background; the Earth should've been twice the size, and there are no stars.
Miriam So?
Martin Well, the moon doesn't have an atmosphere, so the stars should have shone like headlights.
Miriam Why would they have made such a simple mistake?
Martin Well, I suppose if they'd got the position of the stars wrong, then people would have guessed.
Miriam All right, so what else does it say?
Martin You remember the moon buggy?
Miriam I've seen the pictures ...
Martin You need to see the film, but the dust it made as it went along would have taken much longer to fall, you know, come down again, 'cos there's only one sixth of our gravity up there. They can't've been anywhere near the moon. The whole thing must have been filmed in a studio.

Part C

Miriam Well, that's all quite convincing. But there was a rocket launch, wasn't there?
Martin Yeah, but the astronauts weren't on it, were they? They were just hiding somewhere, and then when the rocket came back they were put into the capsule, and dropped into the ocean from a plane!
Miriam But why did they go to so much trouble?
Martin National prestige! The Soviets had put the first man in space, and in 1961, Kennedy had promised to put an American on the moon before the decade was out! But their problem was that their technology wasn't ready.
Miriam You've always got an answer for everything.

27 IT'S MY LIFE

Gerry Have you read this article about the girl who gave up a modelling career?
Martine I have, why?
Gerry I think she's crazy. Why on earth didn't she take it! She could've made millions.
Martine Well, I think it's really nice that she, you know, that being pretty, that it's not the main thing that she wants to show about herself.
Gerry Yes, but even so, she has an opportunity to make a lot of money now which will give her far more choice and freedom later on.
Martine All right, but at the same time if she doesn't value that, so what?
Gerry Yeah, but all the same, if not for herself she ought to have done it for her family. After all, her brother and father were ready to take care of her.
Martine Exploit her, more like!
Gerry Oh, I don't think so ...
Martine Anyway, they look as though they've got enough money at home to live quite comfortably.
Gerry Mind you, you can never have too much ...
Martine Come on ...
Gerry And her dad, he thinks she's crazy, he must've felt sick when she turned the offer down.
Martine What on earth for! He's got no right! It's none of his business. I blame him for talking to the newspapers. He shouldn't've spoken to them in the first place. It's his fault for attracting all this interest.
Gerry That's not fair, he's her dad, he didn't want to see her throw away the chance of a lifetime, that's all.
Martine All right, but the thing is, I really enjoyed school and had a good time, and I think I'd've missed a lot if I hadn't stayed at school, and maybe she thinks that she'd've lost out too.
Gerry I suppose so ... But I bet she'll regret it later on. She should've taken her chance when it was there.

1 Where on earth have you been? It's two o'clock in the morning.
2 What on earth have you done to my CD player? It doesn't work any more!
3 Who on earth is that at the door? We're not expecting visitors.
4 We've missed the last bus. How on earth are we going to get home?
5 She's really upset. Why on earth did you tell her the truth?

28 LIGHTING A CANDLE

Part 1

Miles Joelle Chivers, explain to us why charities spend so much money on advertising.
Joelle Well yes, quite simply they have to. There's so much competition now between different charitable organizations.
Miles Yes, but what we all hate, though, is giving money to help, say, world poverty, knowing half of it is going to rich advertising companies.
Joelle Yes, but without the advertisements and TV commercials, a charity wouldn't stand a chance against its competitors. It's got to build its brand name just like any other business.

Part 2

Miles But don't most of the begging letters they send just end up in the bin unopened? I'm sure lots of us have done this.
Joelle I think it's because people just aren't keen to read about cruelty and misery, especially when it's not close to home.
Miles So people become indifferent?
Joelle That's right. And it's this indifference which is the great fear of all charities. But there are ways to beat it.
Miles Such as ... ?

Part 3

Joelle Well for instance, the organization 'Handicap International', the land mine victims' charity, realized that the first step was to actually get people to open the envelope and look inside.
Miles So what did they do?
Joelle Well, instead of addressing their letters by computer they got the team members in Cambodia to write the addresses by hand and put an ordinary stamp on the letter.
Miles I see, much more personal, so people would get this mysterious letter from Cambodia and be curious ...
Joelle ... that's right, and would at least open it. But they also wanted to get across the idea of what the charity did exactly and to touch people's hearts. So they put into each letter a model of one of the crutches that the victims of land mines use, made from the same materials, so people could literally be 'in touch' with what they were doing.

29 RUMOURS

Part 1

Sandra You'll never guess who I saw in Birmingham.
Roger No, go on.
Sandra Trevor Watson, from Marketing, and he was talking to ... promise you won't tell anyone?
Roger No, of course not. I won't breathe a word.
Sandra Well, he was with Hugh Black from ABC.
Roger No, really? Hugh Black? I don't believe it.
Sandra And they were deep in conversation.
Roger What can it mean, I wonder?
Sandra Well, it must mean he wants Trevor to work for him.

Roger	How interesting! It doesn't surprise me. I've always had my doubts about Trevor. And did Trevor see you?
Sandra	I don't think so, but he looked very suspicious, as though he had something to hide.
Roger	Well, well! You never can tell. I wonder when ...

Part 2

Roger	Alex, hi. Listen, I heard something that might interest you.
Alex	Really? What's that?
Roger	Well, this is in the strictest confidence.
Alex	Yes, of course. My lips are sealed.
Roger	Well, I heard a whisper that Trevor Watson has been headhunted by Hugh Black.
Alex	Headhunted? Well, well.
Roger	Mm, that's what I thought.
Alex	So there'll be a vacancy ... ?
Roger	It might be a good time to have a word with Trevor's boss. You'd be ideal for the job. Anyway, I thought you should be the first to know.

30 TRADING PLACES

Ron	Definitely a bird. I wish I could just grow wings, know what I mean? Something like an eagle. You know, when I was a boy I wanted to join the airforce, to be a pilot, but they weren't interested in me. If I'd studied harder it would have been different, I'm sure. Anyway, that's all in the past now. At weekends I do hang-gliding, and the sensation you get is just incredible. But to be able to fly unaided; that would be really something.
Carmen	If I could be anyone from history, well, I think I would like to have been Queen Isabella. She was alive at such an exciting period, you know, with the discovery of South America and really with the creation of modern Spain. She was marvellous, such a strong character. I wish I could be in charge of my destiny in the same way.
Ian	Well, I've always been interested in keeping fit, but I know, if I'm absolutely truthful, that I haven't got a very good body. I wish I didn't have such short legs. So I think what I would like to be is one of those marvellous Greek statues, you know, of an athlete, a discus thrower maybe. People would wander through the museum and look at my beautiful muscles. They'd be doing that in hundreds of years even. I don't think I'd ever get bored with people admiring me!

31 REPUTATIONS

1

Marcus	Where did you go last night?
Tanya	Out clubbing, you know, like most Saturdays.
Marcus	Who were you with?
Tanya	Mm, the usual friends.
Marcus	Many people there?
Tanya	Yeah, er, it was Saturday night.
Marcus	What time was it when you left?
Tanya	Late. Two-ish, I think.
Marcus	And how did you get home?
Tanya	We managed to get a taxi.

2

Gloria	Hi, I'm so glad to catch you at your desk, it'll only take a minute. Now, I wanted to ask how you felt about these carpet samples, what do you think would go best in the reception area? I'm trying to find out from everyone which one they'd go for, I think it's so important to make the right impression when people come into the building, don't you? And the other one has been looking so scruffy ...

3

John	To the station? Well, er, you turn left out of the building and go down the street, past Marks and Spencer's, they've got a sale on there, I bought a new anorak last Saturday, loads off it, anyway, you go past Marks and then you have to, erm, I think it's turn right by the coffee shop, do you know, I saw Sara in there last week with Jenny, and I waved but they didn't seem to notice me ... so, to the station, yes, you go past Marks and Spencer's...

4

Jenny	Right, I really think we need to make a decision about the party. I thought maybe a boat dinner dance? If we don't book something soon then it'll be too late for anywhere.
Errol	Mmm ... yeah?
Jenny	Though I'm not sure how much people enjoy that sort of thing, the trouble is people can't leave when they want to.
Errol	Um.
Jenny	I was wondering about one of those medieval banquet evenings where people dress up in traditional costume and things. What do you think? ... Hello, is there anybody there?
Errol	Mmm. Dunno really ...

1

Marcus	Hi, Tanya. Where were you yesterday evening?
Tanya	Out clubbing, you know, like most Saturdays.
Marcus	Clubbing again! I don't know where you get your energy from. Did you go with anyone?
Tanya	Mm, the usual friends.
Marcus	Oh right, and I expect it must have been quite crowded?
Tanya	Yeah, erm, it was Saturday night.
Marcus	Of course, I bet you stayed out late then?
Tanya	Yeah, really late! Two-ish, I think.
Marcus	Two o'clock. So it must have been hard to get home?
Tanya	Oh, we were lucky 'cos we managed to get a taxi. I had a really great time.

2

Gloria	Hi, Caroline, I'm so glad to catch you, I know you're terribly busy but I was wondering if you could spare me a minute? I'd really like your opinion ... ?
Caroline	OK then, provided it's only a minute.
Gloria	Oh great, that's really kind of you, you see these carpet samples, what do you think would go best in the reception area ... ?

3

John	To the station? Well, erm, you turn left out of the building and go down the street, past Marks and Spencer's, and then you have to, erm, I think it's turn right by the coffee shop, and then it's straight ahead of you at the bottom. By the way, there's a sale on at Marks at the moment, they've got some good bargains ...

4

Jenny	Right, I really think we need to make a decision about the party. I thought maybe a boat dinner dance? If we don't book something soon then it'll be too late for anywhere.
Errol	So you're saying we should book now? Mm, it is getting late, isn't it.
Jenny	Though I'm not sure how much people enjoy that sort of thing, the trouble is people can't leave when they want to.
Errol	So you think we should do something different?
Jenny	Well, yes, I was wondering about one of those medieval banquet evenings where people dress up in traditional costume and things. What do you think?
Errol	I hear what you're saying but I think we should find out how people would feel about dressing up and so on before we book ...

32 FOLLOW YOUR DREAM

Lots of people have a bright idea but very few are brave enough to **follow** it **through** and **turn** it **into** reality. One of the most courageous stories we've **come across** is that of Leslie Scott, the inventor of *Jenga. Jenga* involves building a tower from 54 wooden blocks, and is extremely tricky. Scott is now rich and successful, but only after **putting up with** years of rejection and uncertainty. She was **brought up** in Africa, and her first language was Swahili. When she was 20, while amusing her young brother, she **came up with** the idea behind *Jenga* which, incidentally, means *to build* in Swahili.

Back in England, Scott **started off** with a job in marketing but decided to **give** it **up** to devote herself to developing the game commercially. She had 1,000 sets made, and looked for a toy maker, but no one was ready to **take** it **on**. Finally, when she was 30, she found one in Canada, and a little money started to come in. However, she was still forced to **take out** bank loans, and when these eventually **ran out**, Scott, now 41, had to sell her house to **pay off** her debts. In 1991, she **set up** her own company, 'Oxford Toys'. Then Scott's luck finally changed; an American toy company **took over** the licence, and in 1993 she made her first big money. Since then, *Jenga* has really **taken off**, and last year, three million people bought it. If it **carries on** being this successful, she'll **end up** by being extremely rich indeed.

OXFORD
UNIVERSITY PRESS

Great Clarendon Street, Oxford OX2 6DP

Oxford University Press is a department of the
University of Oxford. It furthers the University's
objective of excellence in research, scholarship,
and education by publishing worldwide in

Oxford New York

Auckland Cape Town Dar es Salaam
Hong Kong Karachi Kuala Lumpur Madrid
Melbourne Mexico City Nairobi New Delhi
Shanghai Taipei Toronto

With offices in

Argentina Austria Brazil Chile Czech Republic
France Greece Guatemala Hungary Italy Japan
Poland Portugal Singapore South Korea
Switzerland Thailand Turkey Ukraine Vietnam

OXFORD and OXFORD ENGLISH are registered
trade marks of Oxford University Press in the UK
and in certain other countries

© Oxford University Press 2000

The moral rights of the author have been asserted
Database right Oxford University Press (maker)

First published 2000
2009 2008 2007 2006
10 9 8

ISBN-13: 978 0 19 434082 3
ISBN-10: 0 19 434082 1

Printed in China

ACKNOWLEDGEMENTS

*The Publisher and Author would like to thank the following
for their kind permission to use articles, extracts, or
adaptations from copyright material:* Best Magazine and
the author for Suzanne Ostler: 'How I See Myself'
from *Best Magazine*, 31 March 1998.
Moyra Bremner for 'The Art of Conversation' from
*Enquire Within: Modern Etiquette and Successful
Behaviour*, text © 1988, 1990, 1994 (first published
by the Random Century Group 1988, 3rd edition,
Helicon Publishers 1994).
Dell Publishing, a division of Random House, Inc.
for extract from P.J. O'Rourke: 'Flattery' from
Modern Manners (1988).
The Express for article by Simon Young: 'Model
Pupil Who Prefers it at School' from *The Express*,
31 October 1996.
Focus Magazine for 'Mad Days Out' from *Focus*, July
1997.

The Guardian for articles by Kamal Ahmed: 'Holiday
Stereotypes Fall into Sun Trap' from The Guardian,
29 April 1998; and Rosanna Greenstreet: 'He Yong'
from *The Guardian Weekend*, both © The Guardian.
Guinness Publishing for extracts from Geoff
Tibballs: *The Guinness Book of Innovations*, © 1994
Geoff Tibballs and Guinness Publishing.
Charles Handy for 'The Johari Window' from *Inside
Organizations* BBC Books, 1990).
Independent Newspapers (UK) Ltd for articles by
Jeremy Atiyah: 'A Message: Please Ring Jim Haynes
in Paris on 00331 4327 1767' from *The Independent on
Sunday*, 17 May 1998; Shiela Hayman: 'Mesional
Living – Celebration City' from The Independent on
Sunday, 30 June 1996; Gareth Lloyd: 'Where I Grew
Up – Joss Ackland' from *The Independent on Sunday*,
7 September 1997; Tim McGirk: 'Question: Who'd
Want to Spend the Rest of Their Lives Clubbing
Rats?' from *The Independent on Sunday*, 21 November
1993; Cole Moreton: 'How to Make a £49 Million
Cup of Coffee' from *The Independent on Sunday*,
17 May 1998; and Lucy O'Brien: 'What to Wear to
Get That Job' from *The Independent on Sunday*,
10 March 1996.
National Magazine Company Ltd for articles by Sally
Brown: 'Singapore Fixes You Up' from *She*, July 1997,
© She Magazine; Henrietta Holder: 'Things People
Pack' from *Country Living*, February 1995, © Country
Living Magazine; and John Parrish: 'I Think Like a
Serial Killer' from *She*, September 1995, © She
Magazine.
Polarbis Travel Ltd for 'From the Baltic to the Tatras'
from *Polarbis: Poland 1997* brochure.
Solo Syndication Ltd for articles by Lucy Broadbent:
'I pronounce You Man and Woof' from *The Daily
Mail*, 13 April 1996, and Bill Moyland: 'My Little
Cloney' from *The Daily Mail*, 30 June 1996; and
articles from *The Daily Mail*, 27 May 1994 and from
The Mail on Sunday, 6 July 1997.
Time-Life for Greg Burke: 'At Home with Mama'
from *Time*, 7 July 1997, © Time, Inc.
Times Newspapers Limited / News International for
articles by Stuart Wavell: 'Feasting on Fear' from *The
Sunday Times*, 29 June 1997, © Times Newspapers
Limited, 1997; Natalie Graham: 'Towering Success
of a Dogged Toymaker' from *The Sunday Times*, 6 July
1997, © Times Newspapers Limited, 1997; and
extract from article 'A Thousand Makers of The 20th
Century' from *The Sunday Times*, 18 October 1998,
© Times Newspapers Limited 1998.
Time-Life Syndication for Greg Burke: 'At Home
with Mama' from *Time Magazine*, 7 July 1997.
Every effort has been made to trace and contact
copyright holders prior to publication, but in some
cases this has not been possible. We apologize for
any apparent infringement of copyright, and if
notified, the publisher will be pleased to rectify any
errors or omissions at the earliest opportunity.

Illustrations by: Graham Cox pp.22, 68, 82; Trevor
Dunton pp.5, 24, 36, 46; Roger Fereday pp.29, 78;
Nanette Hoogslag/Debut Art cover image; Ian
Jackson pp.14, 21, 25, 30, 35, 40,43, 74, 75, 84, 85,
86, 91, 92, 95, 97, 99, 101, 103, 105, 110, 112; Sarah
Jones p.34; Julian Mosedale pp.18, 38, 54, 80;
Techgraphics OUP pp.15, 87.

Commissioned photography by: Emily Andersen p.33
(Vijay's restaurant) Hadden Davies pp.81 (office
scenes) 83 (woman) Rob Judges pp. 66 (museum), 68
(computer) Mark Mason pp.33 (book / cd cover), 63
(Post-its and Frisbee)

*The Publisher would like to thank the following for their
kind permission to reproduce photographs:* Assignments /
Bryn Colton p.76 (schoolgirl); Associated Press pp.47
(John McConnico), 56 (Greg Baker), 59 (Santiago
Lyon / bull run); Best Magazine p.87; BBC Bristol /

Ruth Flowers pp.10, 11; BMW p.17; Catherine
Blackie p.25; Muriel Bouquet p.90; John Brunton
pp.4, 6; Bubbles pp.14 (Frans Rombout), 17 (Susanna
Price / baby), 26 (Loisjoy Thurstun / friends), 72
(Chris Rout / woman & dog), 83 (James Lamb /
schoolchildren); Camera Press p.83 (Theordore
Wood / Cannes Film Festival); Channel 4 / Windfall
Films p.52; Colorific p.13 (Alon Reininger / Contact),
17 (Arne Hodalic / Saola / puppet), 20 (train); Corbis
pp.39 (Patrick Ward), 53 (Dave Bartruff / tour guide),
53 (Roger Ressmeyer / capsule hotel), 69 (Walter
Hodges), 89 (Underwood & Underwood); Dorling
Kindersley p.59; Mary Evans Picture Library pp.15
(Brigham Young), 40, 65 (Royal Navy / slum); Forge
Mill Needle Museum pp.65, 66; Global Productions
p.28 (courtesy Kobal); Handicap International p.80;
Robert Harding Picture Library pp.11 (Kodak /
woman), (J Bishop / wedding), 12 (Jeff Greenberg),
18 (John Miller), 37 (Statue of Liberty / Big Ben), 111
(cottage); David Hartley p.91; Hulton Getty pp.24,
81; Image Bank pp.23 (Daved de Lossy), 38 (Vital
Picture), 55 (Gk & Vikki Hart), 58 (woman), 61 (Ken
Huang), 71 (Paul Simcock / 'Cathy'), (Romilly
Lockyer / 'Emma'), (David de Lossy / 'Ross'), 75
(Barros & Barros); Impact pp.17 (Tony Page, Oxford),
31 (Simon Shepheard / policeman), 53 (Caroline
Penn / Benidorm disco), 58 (Simon Shepheard /
Sphinx), 60 (John Arthur / Notting Hill Festival,
(John Evans / Venice Carnival), 111 (Caroline Penn /
party); Independent Newspaper / David Sandisan
p.44; Kobal Collection p.31 (car on cliff); Stephen
Lock p.77 (model); Magnum pp.15 (Eve Arnold /
Mormon Choir), 20 (Fred Mayer / Sun City), 50
(Martin Parr), 60 (Richard Kalvar / Naked Festival),
65 (Norman Neason / Forge Mill Needle Museum);
Orion Literary Agency copyright Kenju Kawakami /
International Chindogu Academy p.62; Pittsburg
Gazette p.70 (car burial); Pressens Bild AB p.59
(Mark Maakefelt / Midsommar festival); Eric
Rassmussen p.84; Retna p.48 (Theodore Wood /
Lucinda Lampton); Rex Features pp.9 (Brendan
Deirne / Dracula), (BNP / Tom Payne), 37 (MLW / Bill
Bryson), 48 (Stuart Clarke / Colin Thubron), 53
(Joma Valkonen / Ice Hotel), 70 (John Paul / pet
wedding), 80 (Sipa / Mother Theresa), 86 (Brian
Rasic); Science Photo Library pp.63 (Volker Steger /
velcro), 73 (Nasa / capsule), (Nasa / splashdown);
Telegraph Colour Library pp.26 (VCL / man and car),
83 (David Grossman / Dealing room); Tony Stone
pp.5 (Timothy Shonnad), 7 (Kennan Harvey), 15
(Chuck Pefley / Salt Lake City), (Mark Wagner /
Monument valley), (Bob Torrex / snowboarding), 17
(Cyberimage / football), (Hugh Sitton / Stonehenge),
(Christel Rosenfeld / cheese), (Robert Frerck /
statue), 20 (Alain de Garsmeur / Sark), 31 (Martin
Mouchy / traffic jam), (Mike Magneson / car in
snow), 51 (Images / Peter Timmerman), 57 (Suzanne
& Nick Geary / Holland and Liverpool), (Ulli Seer /
Portugal), 72 (Paul Cheslley / traffic jam), (Donna
Day / boy & TV), (Paul Cherfils / cigarette), 73 (World
Perspectives / lunar buggy), 111 (ski lift), (Nigel
Hillier / Ephesus), (James Strachan / beach).

With additional thanks to Swatch for providing the
watch on p.8.

*The Publisher and Author would like to thank the following
teachers for their help with reading and piloting the
material:* Maria Boguska, Theresa Clementson,
Patrick Creed, Mariza Ferrari, Marek Herda,
Amanda Jeffries, Magdalena Junkieles, John Kay,
Ann Lee, David Massey, Katarzyna Niedzwiecka,
Colin Norris, Jacek Pankrac, Joanna Sosnowska,
Leah Stickley.

The Author would like to thank his family for their
unerring patience and support.